Further Praise for
The Three Laws of Performance

"I believe this book may be one of the most important written in many years. The ideas are much larger than we normally see in business books. They aren't tips, tools, or steps, but are in fact laws that govern individual, group, and organizational behavior. In striving for what's possible, not just for what's likely, this book can be a resource for generations to come."

From the Editor's Note by Warren Bennis

"God invites each of us to participate in the process of transforming the world—to create a world in which every person knows their infinite and irreplaceable worth and can truly fulfill their potential. This book, filled with insights, real-life encounters and experiences, shows us **how** we may do this work of transformation. Applicable in the corporate, labor, political, and civil society sectors—Steve and Dave have written an inspiring, practical book that will assist all who seek to rewrite the future of our world."

Archbishop Emeritus Desmond Tutu, Nobel Laureate

"The world needs this book; it is a gem. The ideas and stories presented are empowering tributes to leaders and organizations who create space for success."

Paul Fireman, founder, Reebok International; now chairman, Fireman Capital Partners, Boston and New York

"I am the founder of a fast-growing public company that has surfed the backbone of the ideas in this book, and I attribute much of our success to applying them. When we realized that the company was operating in silos, we used applications derived from *The Three Laws of Performance* to have cross-functional teams create exciting, aligned futures that have resulted in unprecedented business results."

Chip Wilson, founder, lululemon athletica

"This book is filled with powerful illustrations that show what organizations and individuals can do to make the world work. It gives hope to leaders at all levels."

Jack Canfield, coauthor, *The Success Principles*™ and the *Chicken Soup for the Soul*® series

"I invite all readers to be open to what may occur as an unfamiliar and perhaps even strange way to think about people and organizational issues. There is much to learn and the payoffs are huge."

From the Foreword by Michael Jensen, Jesse Isidor Straus Professor of Business, Emeritus, Harvard Business School

"For a person in a leadership position or someone aspiring to take a leadership position this is a worthwhile read. As a compendium of relevant experience, it will be hard to beat."

Sir Bob Reid, chairman, International Petroleum Exchange, former chairman and chief executive, Shell UK

"At the Anthony Robbins' Companies we have a huge commitment to people achieving total peak performance and optimum results in life. This book delineates the laws that allow people, companies, and organizations to create these unprecedented results. The thinking is novel and nothing short of brilliant."

Sam Georges, CEO and president, Anthony Robbins Holdings

"This is an amazing book! It captures the principles behind applications and processes that were implemented with most of the 15,000 employees I managed within Telemar, Brazil's largest telecommunications company. One year after the start of that process, the company successfully entered a growing and profitable new market. In my view, without the ideas in this book, we never would have gotten there that fast. It was the most exciting adventure of my life."

Marcio Roza, former CEO, Telemar Rio

"By applying the Three Laws I noticed an instant transformation in all areas of my life. In business, sport, and relationships, I was able to rewrite my future, which is now full of endless possibilities."

Natalie Cook, four-time Olympian, Australian Beach Volleyball Team; gold medalist, Sydney, 2000

"Steve Zaffron and Dave Logan have produced a book which illustrates how companies, and people, carry through the kind of transformation that occurs when water turns into steam or into ice. If you're only interested in mediocrity, in water that's a little warmer or a little colder, this book won't matter to you. But if you really want to create your own future, the numerous real-life examples they give and the crystal-clear explanations they use to make their experience available to us are essential. How would I know? Well, I guess it's because I was able to survive 16 years in wrongful solitary confinement in Chinese prisons and emerge to enjoy a Hollywood happy ending, primarily because I followed the basic laws that this book illuminates to dissolve my 'default future' and create a new future for myself. It's what works—really!"

Sidney Rittenberg, founder, Rittenberg Associates; consultant on business relations in China; coauthor, *The Man Who Stayed Behind*

"This book is a perfect combination of fine storytelling and rock-solid ideas. It makes accessible a powerful way of thinking which has the capacity to transform businesses and their communities. I definitely recommend you read this book."

Peter Block, author, *Community: The Structure of Belonging*

"In this thoughtful book, Steve Zaffron and Dave Logan show how leadership can be nurtured through becoming more aware of some fundamental laws that govern human behavior and thereby organizational outcomes. Those who aspire for more joyful and productive ways to lead their lives and organizations will find it to be an invaluable read."

Mark Zupan, dean, Simon School of Business, University of Rochester

"This book is one of a kind. It explains how life truly works, offering, as it were, a view of the elephant in all its glory, not merely the tusk or the tail. Included are instructions that are guaranteed to boost performance in ways that are utterly unexpected and wholly reliable. One gets the impression that having discovered the secret of life, the authors have a deep and genuine desire to share it with their readers."

Rosamund Zander, coauthor, *The Art of Possibility*

"I have seen and witnessed the power of this realization in a dusty mining community in post Apartheid South Africa, where thousands of South Africans said that *together* their future would be written differently, creatively. Practicing the principles as outlined in this profound and readable book, a whole community was empowered to become the *space* for a transformed future.

This book isn't about ideas and theories; it is about the rugged hard work of writing a different future for you, your community, your company or organization—a future that is inclusive, alive, possible, and sustainable. It's the only future we have.

I acknowledge Steve and Dave for their unique and exceptional contribution and for showing us *how* to do this work. It couldn't come at a more momentous time."

The Reverend Chris Ahrends, former chaplain to Archbishop Desmond Tutu, CEO, Four Consulting, South Africa

The Three Laws of Performance gives access to being a person of integrity and an extraordinary leader. Using the ideas in this book, you will see that there are no limits to what you can achieve."

Richard V. De Mulder, professor, Erasmus University, Rotterdam, Netherlands

"At the end of the day when you implement solutions identified in a Six Sigma and/or Lean project, your ability to execute the solution is not dependent on the set of technical tools. It is people embracing the solution and acting on it. This is a book that will help you understand and respect the importance of language and how it can be used to leverage communication into a powerful business improvement tool."

Mike Carnell, coauthor, *Leaning Into Six Sigma*, president and CEO, CS International, LP

"*The Three Laws of Performance* is a fascinating book that will change your perspective on your organization, your people, and on yourself. Through a combination of a deep, practical, and often philosophical understanding of what it is to be human, a wide range of telling examples, and a set of exercises, this book has the rare capacity of delivering insights that ring home and will make a difference. Our personal experience is that this not only generates new and unprecedented opportunities but does so through passion and joy of play."

Jaap Winter, partner, De Brauw Blackstone Westbroek
Kees Cools, executive director,
The Boston Consulting Group in Amsterdam
Principals, Wintercools corporate governance advisors

"Great performance is about people. *The Three Laws of Performance* gets to the heart of how leaders learn about their employees, their organization, and themselves. You will have a clearer understanding of how you can unlock the power of people when you are done reading this book."

Garry Ridge, president and CEO, WD-40 Company

The Three Laws of Performance

Warren Bennis

A WARREN BENNIS BOOK

This collection of books is devoted exclusively to new and exemplary contributions to management thought and practice. The books in this series are addressed to thoughtful leaders, executives, and managers of all organizations who are struggling with and committed to responsible change. My hope and goal is to spark new intellectual capital by sharing ideas positioned at an angle to conventional thought—in short, to publish books that disturb the present in the service of a better future.

Books in the Warren Bennis Signature Series

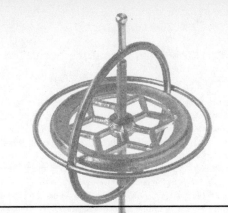

The Three Laws of
Performance

Rewriting the Future of Your
Organization and Your Life

Steve Zaffron
and Dave Logan

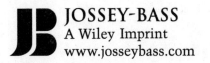

JOSSEY-BASS
A Wiley Imprint
www.josseybass.com

Published by Jossey-Bass.
A Wiley Imprint
989 Market Street, San Francisco, CA 94103-1741—www.josseybass.com

Jossey-Bass books and products are available through most bookstores. To contact Jossey-Bass directly call our Customer Care Department within the U.S. at 800-956-7739, outside the U.S. at 317-572-3986, or fax 317-572-4002.

Jossey-Bass also publishes its books in a variety of electronic formats. Some content that appears in print may not be available in electronic books.

Library of Congress Cataloging-in-Publication Data

Zaffron, Steve, 1944-
   The three laws of performance : rewriting the future of your organization
and your life / Steve Zaffron and Dave Logan.
         p. cm.
   Includes bibliographical references and index.
   ISBN 978-0-470-19559-8 (cloth)
   1. Performance. 2. Organization. 3. Leadership. I. Logan,
David (David Coleman) II. Title.
   BF481.Z23 2009
   650.1—dc22

                                                      2008044975

Printed in the United States of America

FIRST EDITION

HB Printing   10 9 8 7 6 5 4 3 2 1

Contents

We dedicate this book to our wives, Olga and Harte,
who kept our dream alive, even when we forgot it.

Editor's Note

There must be a Jay Gatsby gene in all of us who are involved in the improbable task of transforming organizations. F. Scott Fitzgerald's Gatsby, our avatar, embodied this with his "passion for the promises of life." I've been brooding and thinking about this for more than a half century, and at times I think it's a bootless chase; in more promising moods, a Sisyphean task; and at other times, one of Zeus's cruel hoaxes he pulls on us susceptible mortals from time to time to prod us further in search of a vivid utopia. Then every once in a while a book comes along with a jolt that uplifts and restores your simmering passion and brings it to a boil. This book of Zaffron and Logan does just that. And I'm still happily surprised that they managed to pull it off.

I first heard their ideas, several years ago, in a quietly elegant restaurant in Santa Monica. I listened to them with equal amounts of wonder and skepticism. What fascinated me that evening, most of all, was their gutsy aspiration: to integrate an interdisciplinary slew of disciplines as disparate as brain science, linguistics, organizational theory, and complex adaptive systems with a few fundamental laws of human and organizational behavior that could lead to palpable and profound change in both domains. That's a mouthful—and hearing about this for the first time, I tried unsuccessfully to suspend my disbelief. So I asked them to write it up. Words do have a way with me, and I needed a lot more assurance than words thrown about in a star-kiss'd evening over too many drinks. That was five years ago.

Since then, I worked with Steve and Dave, reviewing one draft after the other. There's something to be said for wallowing and marinating, and with each draft my enthusiasm mounted. I wasn't quite the midwife to this book; *godfather* better describes my role.

I believe this book may be one of the most important written in many years. The ideas are much larger than what we normally see in business books. They aren't tips, tools, or steps, but are in fact laws that govern individual, group, and organizational behavior. The stories aren't the normal ones we read about in business; rather, they are illustrations of organizations bringing out the best in people and in communities. These aren't just companies making a profit, but companies doing well in the world, by any measure. Leaders would be well served to think about these laws and find ways to apply their insights.

Working through this book, the reader will have an advantage that I didn't have when I first listened to Steve and Dave. The reader can pause, think, reflect. Even set the book down and talk about it with others. Then go back and continue on. I found the stories in the book to be like movies, ones that surprised me in their poignancy. I keep recalling the pictures and images of the different cultures and companies in the book and the people who struggled to make new realities happen. For me, the most surprising, improbable, and inspiring are the glimpses into the world of Lonmin, the platinum mining company in South Africa. As many times as I've read the story through various drafts over the years, it still inspires me about what organizations can become, and should become.

Chapter Five, on self-led organizations, is rich for a different reason. It paints a vision of what organizations can become, in which the organization itself becomes a leader in the world. That chapter is paradigm-busting, and I hope business leaders will go through it slowly and with reflection.

As we move into the heart of the twenty-first century, it's time for business leaders to ask what impact they want their career and their entire organization to make. The future that's already written about organizations is not the most ideal. We can do better; we must do better. In helping us to strive for what's possible, not just for what's likely, this book can be a resource for generations to come.

Warren Bennis
December 2008

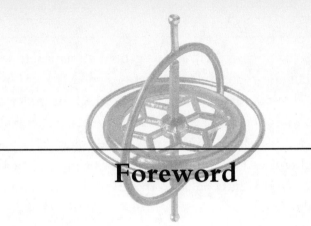

Foreword

I have no doubt that the ideas, distinctions, and methodologies that underlie what Steve and Dave so expertly present will have a substantial impact on the world. I'm honored to be invited to write this foreword.

When I was first introduced to some of the ideas contained in this book I saw the extraordinary impact they made on the audience. I was struck by the enormous potential, relevance, and applicability of this approach to transforming human beings and organizations. But from my worldview I could not understand how this dramatic impact occurred. Since then I have spent considerable time and energy researching these ideas on my own and in collaboration with Steve and Dave with the intention to see them become universally available. It has not been a simple task. This book takes a substantial step toward accomplishing this aspiration. My congratulations!

I contacted Steve early in my efforts to get to the bottom of these ideas and to fully grasp their ability to dramatically influence the power and productivity of people and organizations. Much of my research and writing is now devoted to these efforts. In 1997 I was hitting the wall as a leader with my Faculty Unit at the Harvard Business School. To be blunt I was failing. I asked Steve to help and he generously agreed to work with me and my group (the Organizations and Markets Group at HBS). That two days of work (during which he undertook a task that most of us thought impossible in such a short time) put us, as a group, back on the track to becoming a formally sanctioned unit of HBS. For that, and for being the teacher, counselor, partner, and colleague that Steve has been for me, I am deeply grateful.

Steve has a proven track record over decades of designing and implementing large-scale initiatives that elevate organizational performance, and that talent was truly required to bring the Organizations and Markets Group at HBS to its current status. In addition to witnessing his successful work with my group, I've been fortunate to both observe and work with Steve in designing and delivering programs in other client and academic settings. He is a master.

I met Dave Logan through the Barbados Group (see Authors' Note). Dave has deep expertise in researching and designing programs that synthesize organizational change, management, and leadership. I have been privileged to work with him in delivering sessions of an executive development program for a large multinational company. I am always amazed at Dave's ability to penetrate to the core of what it takes to bring about progress. I recall one particularly difficult situation I faced when Dave coached and guided me in a way that quickly turned this situation around. Dave is also a master.

I must recognize the members of the Barbados Group; in particular, Werner Erhard, for being the catalyst that brought these extraordinary thinkers together and for his superb leadership of the group's discussions. I am deeply grateful for the contribution these conversations have made to me personally and to this book.

I especially invite all readers to be open to what may occur as an unfamiliar and perhaps even strange way to think about people and organizational issues.

There is much to learn and the payoffs are huge.

Michael C. Jensen
Jesse Isidor Straus, Professor of Business Emeritus
Harvard Business School
Sharon, Vermont
September 2008

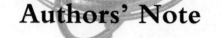

Authors' Note

This book stems from a unique partnership, and it wouldn't have been possible without input from an extraordinary group of individuals.

Steve has been called a "Zen Master in a business suit," and Dave has the nickname "Dr. Phil to the Fortune 500." In the 1960s, Steve was getting his education, both in grad school and on the streets of Chicago, around the time that Dave was born.

Somehow, in the course of our very different lives, we both became passionate around the same question: How do people perform beyond their limits?

Steve's involvement with this question started thirty years ago, when he first met Werner Erhard, the founder of *est* and originator of transformational ideas and applications. Today, Steve is the CEO of Vanto Group and has worked with more than a hundred thousand people and a wide range of businesses, in over twenty countries. In addition, Steve is an executive and board member with Vanto's parent company, Landmark Education, where he spearheaded the development of Landmark's programs. Today, Landmark has over a million graduates.

Dave took a very different journey. After becoming an associate professor at the Marshall School of Business at the University of Southern California, and one of the youngest associate deans in the institution's history, he wanted to play a more direct role in making businesses work. Today, Dave balances teaching at the Marshall School of Business with consulting to many of the Fortune 500 companies as a senior partner in CultureSync.

We first met ten years ago when Dave invited Steve to lecture to his graduate business class at USC. During that first meeting, Dave proposed writing a case study that would highlight the impact of what Steve had developed in applying transformation in a corporate setting. When that case study broke sales records, we realized there was a demand for these ideas far beyond what we had originally thought.

Around the time of that realization, we joined with about a dozen academics, corporate executives, and consultants to examine the impact of personal and organizational transformation. This group, which became known as the Barbados Group after the location of our first meeting, investigated situations in which performance surpassed expectations and then studied the theories that might explain these surprising results. In the course of its work, the group reviewed models from brain science, linguistics, complex adaptive systems, philosophy, many other disciplines, as well as ideas from the oral tradition of *est* and Landmark Education. From this inquiry, a new model of performance emerged.

Several years into the process, the Barbados Group felt an urgency to get these ideas out to a wide audience. This book is a first step toward that end.

To say we are indebted to our fellow members is an understatement, as everything we write here stems from their hard work, relentless focus, and fierce commitment to produce a model of performance that would make a real difference in business and in the lives of people.

The members of the Barbados Group are Sir Christopher Ball, Patron, Talent Foundation, and former chancellor, University of Manchester; Peter Block, author, and business and community consultant; Allan Cohen, strategy consultant; Joseph DiMaggio, director of research and development, Landmark Education, and former research physician, Memorial Sloan-Kettering Research Center; Werner Erhard, creator of transformational ideas and applications; Bruce Gregory, Harvard-Smithsonian Center for Astrophysics Science Education; Michael Jensen, senior advisor, the Monitor Company, and Harvard Business School Professor Emeritus; Olga Loffredi, managing director, Vanto Group Latin America; Brad Mills, former CEO, Lonmin Plc.; Robert Rosen, psychologist, author, and chairman and CEO, Healthy Companies International; Harry Rosenberg, CEO, Landmark Education Enterprises; Allan Scherr, management consultant, and former IBM Fellow and Vice President; Michael Zimmerman, professor and director, Center for Humanities and the Arts, University of Colorado, Boulder; Mark Zupan, dean, Simon School of Business, University of Rochester; and both authors of this book.

This book pools contributions from many difference sources: the Barbados Group; Steve's time with Landmark Education and the Vanto Group; Dave's teaching, research, and consulting through USC and CultureSync; and the thousands of people we've worked with over several decades.

The result: Three Laws that provide concise, elegant access to elevating performance far above what most of us think is possible.

Introduction: The Power of Rewriting the Future

In our work lives, when something isn't working, we struggle with which part of the problem to tackle first. Do we start with cost reduction? What about morale? Or should we begin with process improvement?

In our personal lives, it's the same dilemma—which problem do we work on first? Should we resolve to do better with home finances? Make our marriage more fulfilling? Get rid of ten pounds? Spend more time with the kids?

The optimist says there's opportunity everywhere we look. The pessimist says everything is messed up, and it's as though every system is perfectly designed to stay messed up, no matter how many things we try to fix.

We pick the problem to work on, and we either fail or succeed. If we fail, we add "frustration" to our list of problems. If we succeed, a new problem pops up to replace the old one. The solution to a problem becomes the next problem. We cut 10 percent out of our department budget, and our star performers leave in frustration, experiencing a lack of support for projects important to them. We quit smoking and gain ten pounds. We go to the gym to lose the weight, and our family complains we're not home enough. We spend more time at home, and our boss gripes that we're not getting enough done, the budget is out of control, and when are we going to fire the next person we can't afford to lose? It's so much stress that, before we know it, we're smoking again.

It's as though the system we're working on—the company, finances, health, our personal life—is an old inner tube. The moment we patch one hole and add pressure, another spot rips open.

People spend their lives perfecting the art of improvement—more, better, different, and faster. Using this approach, many problems seem intractable.

As the French proverb says, the more things change, the more they stay the same. Why is that?

Imagine a company that is missing its financial targets, selling products people aren't buying. The cubicles are packed with frustrated people who take their malaise home. Dissatisfaction spills out into family life and, through the employees' children, into the schools and community. If we try to fix this problem in patchwork style, we may never get ahead of the corporate death spiral. Create new products, only to find investors have pulled out. Work on financial reporting—as the competition releases a new product that puts ours further behind.

The reason fixing problems often doesn't deliver expected results is that the result is only superficial. What's left untouched are the underlying dynamics that perpetuate the problem.

For every "problem," there is a future that's already been written about it. This future includes people's assumption, hopes, fears, resignation, cynicism, and "lessons learned" through past experience. Although this future is almost never talked about, it is the context in which people try to create change.

If you went into the company described earlier, and got employees talking about the future, they'd probably say something like *It will never work out. We're mired in politics, so when we do bring a product to market, it's two years too late, and that's not going to change. Our leaders will never lead—it's not in them. We'll just waste away until we're bought or shut down.*

Although most people have never articulated what they *really* think will happen to them personally or organizationally, they live every moment as if it's destined to come about. Employees are reduced to going through the motions, never fully engaging, never taking on the politics that they believe is holding the company back.

If you interviewed the leaders in this company, you'd hear a future that is correlated with what the employees describe, something like *People here don't care, and they never will. We invite their ideas, but they never come through with anything good. We don't have the money to replace them with star performers, and so we'll always be a B player in this industry at best. We'll continue to do the best we can, but as a company, we'll never really succeed.*

Like the employees, the leaders do their best in a situation that is doomed to mediocrity. They ask employees for input, already thinking to themselves that the suggestions will be second-rate. Leaders work hard, but the company continues to lose ground against the competitors. People at all levels are frustrated but don't see anything they can do to help.

Two points are critical here. First, everyone experiences a future in front of them, even though few could articulate it. It goes beyond what they expect to happen, hope will happen, or think might happen. This future lives at a gut level. We *know* it's what will happen, whether we can give words to it or not.

We call this the *default future*, and every person has one. So does every organization.

Second, people's relationship with the default future is complex. If someone described your default future to you, you might disagree, perhaps even get angry at how different that future is from what you think will happen. (Remember, the default future lives at an experiential level. It's underneath what we think and hope will happen.) Yet you (along with the rest of us) live as if that future is preordained. You live into your default future, unaware that by doing so you are making it come about.

To see the complexity at work, think about people you know who have wrestled with the same personal problem for years—weight, drugs, alcohol, or an unhappy personal relationship. Although they might say, "I want to get help," or "this will be different," their actions show a recurrence. Why is it so hard to change? Because wrestling with that problem, over and over, lives in their future—sometimes winning, sometimes losing, but always struggling. No matter how much they try to change, or how many self-help books they read, their default future has a predictable shape.

The same dynamic exists at the organizational level. Statistical evidence shows that most significant change efforts fail. The reason for this is that regardless of the management interventions tried, the default futures of employees and leaders are still in place. The more things change, the more they stay the same.

This book isn't about change management—more, better, or different. It's about rewriting the future. The result is the transformation of a situation, leading to a dramatic elevation in performance.

Imagine, in the example we presented, what the company would look like if the people rewrote their future. What if it were this: *We've turned around the company. We have come from behind and set the standard for the industry. We are people that work together, innovate, and succeed.*

Notice that we're not talking about motivational speeches or slogans that people repeat. We're talking about rewriting what people *know* will happen. Rewrite this future, and people's actions naturally shift: from disengaged to proactive, from resigned to inspired, from frustrated to innovative. If we could rewrite the future across a critical mass of people, we could transform a tired company into an innovator, a burned-out culture into one of inspiration, a command-and-control structure into a system in which everyone pulls for each other's success. This kind of transformation creates a wave of momentum: investors want in, companies want to partner with us, potential employees want to join our ranks.

Notice that all this happened without targeting the problems themselves. Rewrite the future, and old problems disappear.

After reading this book, you will see how to rewrite your future and the future of an entire organization. Applying the ideas here will produce levels of performance many people believe is impossible.

Seem far-fetched? This book is filled with examples that are this dramatic.

The power in this book stems from using the Three Laws of Performance. A law isn't a rule, tip, or step; it distinguishes the moving parts at play behind an observable phenomenon. A law is invariable. Whether you believe in gravity or not doesn't lessen its effect on you.

The greatest advances in history have come from applying newly discovered laws. Think of Newton's three laws of motion. Each on its own is interesting and insightful, and when combined together and applied, they become powerful and predictive.

When the Three Laws in this book are applied, performance transforms to a level far beyond what most people think is possible. It doesn't happen bit by bit, but all at once, as individuals and organizations rewrite their future.

Part One (Chapters One, Two, and Three) takes these laws, one at a time, and shows how to apply them. You'll see how to jettison what's holding you back and create a future for your business and your life beyond what's predictably going to happen. Along the way, you'll likely see and transform much of what is holding you back, both professionally and personally.

Through the journey of these first three chapters, we'll visit companies in South Africa, Japan, South America, and the United States, looking into diverse industries such as aerospace, energy, construction, and mining. We'll make stops in a high-tech start-up, a major Brazilian oil company, even the Harvard Business School. We'll see that the Three Laws always hold—they are universal principles that apply any time human beings are involved in any kind of effort. We'll see the result of understanding and applying them—dramatic elevations in performance.

Part Two (Chapters Four and Five) looks at leadership in light of the Three Laws. This section identifies key leadership principles and how to apply them in organizations. We also look at the new frontier of organizations: working effectively in the developing world, creating sustainability in communities, and generating the expansion of wealth (both material and in the well-being of people). This section is intended for people interested in organizational leadership. If your interest is mostly personal application, you may want to skip to Part Three.

Part Three (Chapters Six, Seven, and Eight) is about the personal face of leadership. Chapter Six shows how you can apply the Three Laws to yourself—and in the process expand your own leadership. Chapter Seven is about taking the walk down the path to mastery of the Three Laws. Chapter Eight offers some guidance on how to take these new ideas out into your world.

This book is not an academic study, although its conclusions draw on well-established lines of research. Our intent is to introduce these laws and illustrate how their application can enhance performance. The examples almost all come from cases in which we and our colleagues have been personally involved. We've been there, we've seen it, and now we want to share it.

In reading this book and applying the Three Laws, you'll do more than find fixes to your problems. You'll find the power to rewrite your future.

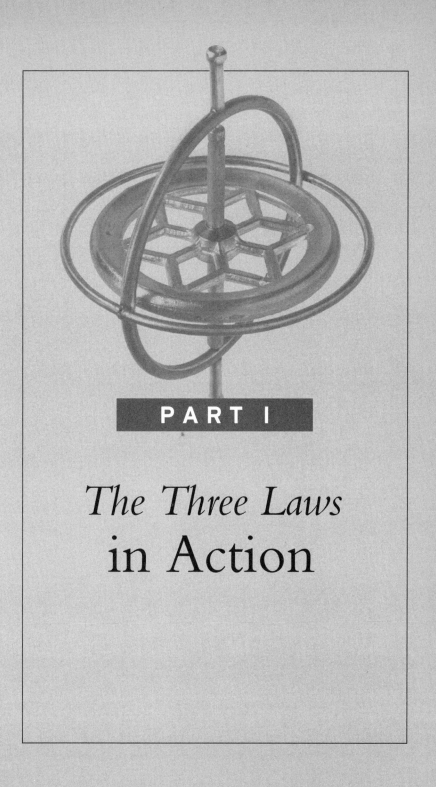

PART I

The Three Laws
in Action

1

Transforming an Impossible Situation

Two hours northwest of Johannesburg, just off the Platinum Highway, is an abandoned archeological dig with a sign that bears the words, "Cradle of Humanity." The communities nearby are home to the platinum mining operations of Lonmin Plc., the world's third-largest producer of the precious metal. These nine communities and five squatter camps, of approximately three hundred thousand people, are also where we find many people who fought—and are still fighting—for Nelson Mandela's vision of a new South Africa. In this most unlikely of places, less than ten years after the end of apartheid, a conversation took place that shows the power of the First Law of Performance—the subject of this chapter.

Antoinette Grib, a white South African senior manager of Lonmin, was speaking to a group of about one hundred people when an elderly community member stood up, interrupted, and insisted on saying something to her. The woman, Selinah Makgale, began: "Antoinette, I have an issue with you."

Grib's shock was obvious. She said, "But I don't even know you."

Makgale continued, "Yes, I don't know you personally, but you are a white South African woman, and I have an issue with white South African women. When I was thirteen years old, my parents told me that I needed to be the housekeeper for the white Afrikaans that owned the farm we worked on. It was payment for us working the farm. I was like a slave, not earning a cent. The woman, she was very, very bad to me. Getting through that year was tough. I've been hating white South African women ever since."

Makgale paused, then continued, "I'm sorry, even though I don't know you, I've been sitting here for days hating you and all the other South African women. You probably weren't even born when all this happened."

Grib smiled and said, "No, I wasn't."

After another thoughtful moment, Makgale finished with: "Please accept my apology—you and all the other white South African women here. I apologize to you all for making you a faceless group and hating you."

Some people became serious, others looked like they were remembering the past. Some shook their heads. All were visibly touched by Makgale's courage and intent to close a chapter from the past.

The senior manager took the next step, saying,

Selinah, I see that I represent something to you with my blond hair and my blue eyes that caused so much pain in your life all those years ago. I ask your forgiveness for the mistakes my people made. . . . I think we're fortunate to live in a country now, since 1994, where we can move forward and we can live together. I offer you my support in getting this issue completely resolved. If you want, I will go with you to visit the woman who treated you so poorly and see if there are some amends that can be made. We can try that.

Both women started to cry—one elderly, poor, and black, and one young, wealthy, and white. Makgale replied, "Yes, I am willing to do that. Thank you very much. I hope our future can grow better than before." The group cheered.

If these two individuals worked together every day, what difference would this exchange have made in their performance?

What if conversations like this were common, in your company, family, and life?

In part because interactions like this one are frequent around Lonmin, relationships with the community are unusually positive. Inside Lonmin, conversations don't have the same noise of gossip and distraction that are business as usual in the world. People act with greater focus, more collaboration, less distraction.

Lonmin elevates its performance.

This book is about performance, and the Three Laws that govern it. In the pages that follow, we will ask you to think in new ways, to examine old assumptions, and explore new ways of approaching old situations. If you do, our promise to you is breakthrough performance in your organization and your life.

At times, we'll invite you to think, inquire, reflect, and, in some cases, consider discussing topics with other people. It's fine to skip through these sections and return to them later when convenient. But dealing with these sections at some point will produce benefits for you.

It's useful, to start, for you to pick an area in your business or life that would benefit from a breakthrough in performance. What you pick may not immediately look to you like a performance challenge—it may look like something else, such as complaints you have with your company's culture, or difficulties in implementing new initiatives, or just plain conflicts in relationships at work or in life.

It may be something as simple as a commitment that never gets realized, like a New Year's resolution that you make over and over to no avail. But if you ask yourself, "Why do I care about this issue being resolved?" you'll find that this issue is something that gets in the way of producing results and accomplishment—that is, performance. To the degree that the issue you choose is one that really matters to you, you'll get that much more out of the sections that follow.

The First Law of Performance

How people perform correlates to how situations occur to them.

The First Law answers the question, "Why do people do what they do?" Although there are countless books, theories, and models on this topic, most provide explanations but don't directly alter performance. The First Law, on the other hand, gives the leverage that the rest of this book will capitalize on. Consider that when *we* do something, it always makes complete sense to *us*. On the other hand, when *others* do something, we often question, "Why are they doing that? It doesn't make any sense!" But if we got into the world of the person, and looked at how the situation occurred to him, we would experience that the same actions that we were questioning were completely and absolutely the perfect and correct thing for him to do, given how the situation is occurring to the person. Each person assumes that the way things occur for him or her is how they are occurring for another. But situations occur differently for each person. Not realizing this can make another's actions seem out of place.

So what exactly does *occur* mean? We mean something beyond perception and subjective experience. We mean the reality that arises within and from your perspective on the situation. In fact, your perspective is itself part of the way in which the world occurs to you. "How a situation occurs" includes your view of the past (why things are the way they are) and the future (where all this is going).

Although there certainly are facts about how and why things are the way they are, the facts of the matter are much less important to us than the way those facts occur to us. The First Law rejects the commonsense view of actions—that people do what they do in a situation because of a common understanding of the facts.

What gives the First Law the potential to alter performance is its relationship to the other two laws. At the risk of getting ahead of ourselves, we will show in the next two chapters that "the way a situation occurs" to people, and their correlated performance, can be altered through a certain use of language.

Given the different positions that well-informed, intelligent people often take on a situation, there is a significant difference between the objective facts of the matter and the way those facts occur to each of us. Again, we are not saying that there isn't a "real world." We are merely pointing out that our actions relate to how the world occurs to us, not to the way that it actually is.

When people relate to each other as if each is dealing with the same set of facts, they have fallen into the *reality illusion*. To see the reality illusion at work, think of a person you aren't happy with at the moment—perhaps someone you've been resenting for years. In your own mind, think of words that describe that person.

You might say, "self-centered," "doesn't listen," "opinion-ated," and "irrational." You might be willing to swear on a stack of bibles that those words are accurate. But notice that you've described how the person *occurs* to you. As human beings, we can almost never see the occurring as an occurring. What we see is just the way it is.

Consider: How would that person describe you? Or in the terms we are using here, how do you occur for him? Perhaps "opinionated," "angry," and "resentful." Perhaps some other way. When you look at it, often you see that we have very little experience of how we occur for others.

We're not suggesting that either of you is right or wrong, but rather pointing out the reality illusion at work. None of us sees things as they are. We see how things occur to us.

Before the exchange between the two women in South Africa, Antoinette Grib occurred to Selinah Makgale as untrustworthy, provoking anger and resentment.

What happened in this exchange is that Makgale identified and altered how Grib occurred to her. As she did, her actions toward the senior manager shifted, from cold anger to possible friendship. The First Law says that how a situation, or in this case a person, occurs goes hand in hand with action. The actions included an embrace and a promise of future action.

Consider the issues in your life, those parts of your life that aren't working. Consider issues at work and at home. Think about the performance challenge you identified earlier. You will take a big step toward transforming them—not merely trying to change them—if you see that you aren't seeing them as they are. The reality illusion will try to convince you that you are. But just as it is for the rest of us, what looks like reality is only how reality occurs to you.

This First Law, then, says that there are two elements: performance and how a situation occurs. These two are perfectly matched, *always*, with no exceptions.

The First Law and the Future

Another employee of Lonmin is Laolang Phiri, who lives in the nearby community of Marikana.

Laolang, muscular and of average height, looks like a running back for a college football team. He has bright eyes and a proud bearing. His open spirit stands in sharp contrast to his local origins—a shantytown where, even today, 40 percent of the population in his community are unemployed and 80 percent live in shacks.

When most mining companies opened their mines decades ago, they began a practice still standard today: recruiting employees from other countries—Zimbabwe, Mozambique, and Zambia. It's commonplace for these foreign workers to leave their families for months at a time and live in single-sex hostels—some finding themselves on the "all dark" shift: spending the daylight hours 3,500 feet underground in the dark, returning to the surface at night.

A too common casualty are the men who end up resorting to drugs, alcohol, and visits to the local prostitutes. Until recently, the government took little effective action against AIDS, and the disease is now rampant within the community. Some 25 percent of Lonmin's twenty-five thousand employees test positive for HIV, and sixty-seven people from its workforce died of AIDS-related diseases in 2005.

On one of our visits, we entered Laolang's workplace by straddling T-chairs on what looked like a ski lift. But instead of going up, we descended at a 30-degree angle into the earth. As we went deeper, darkness took over. Behind us was a string of workers, one per chair, some smoking, visible only by the lights on their miners' hard hats. The air was hot from blasting and wet from the water that cools the drills, with a sticky residue of explosives. The area was lit by strings of bare bulbs, just enough light so workers don't trip on the machinery that lines the passageways. This is Laolang's world.

If you think of doing this every day, for years at a time, with your family far away, it's not surprising that Laolang, like many of his fellow workers, was frustrated and angry about the quality of his life, and blamed the mine management.

"The union thought that management sees them only as tools," he told us. "We didn't feel like people, but some things that they brought in to do the work, that's replaceable. The managers were like, 'We own this mine, and we're not going to be pushed around by the tools.'"

"It was blacks versus whites, all the time," he continued. "If you're black, you're a worker. If you're in a senior position, you're white. And if somehow a black person ends up in a senior position, they must have sold out and turned white," he laughed.

"We felt the white unions got whatever they demanded, and we really had a problem with that," he said, with his inviting smile fading a bit. Laolang paused, clenched his teeth, and then summarized: "I was angry all the time. I knew the future would be a constant fight." Laolang had channeled his feelings into action by becoming a union representative.

Laolang wasn't alone in his anger. In 2004, a local university team of researchers studied perceptions about Lonmin throughout the communities that surround it and concluded the mine was a ticking time bomb of public rage.

Because of how situations occurred to Laolang, his future was already written, as was that of his union, his community, and his employer. The future would be a constant struggle, a fight for dignity and fair pay. It would be that way until he died, just as it had been for generations in South Africa.

The future is already written because, as the First Law says, people's performance will always correlate with how situations occur to them. Until the occurring shifts, as it did for the two women at the start of the chapter, the future is established, and people's actions are on a direct path to making that future come about.

A Surprising Turn of Events

In 2004, Laolang's life intersected with someone from a different world: Brad Mills, the newly appointed CEO of Lonmin. A direct descendant of the Vanderbilt family, he was determined to make his own mark in the world. After studying geology and economics at Stanford, he became an exploration geologist in search of ores in remote parts of the world. Now in his fifties, six foot two, his dark hair streaked with gray, he has the bearing of an Indiana Jones, and his eyes gleam when he talks about Lonmin becoming a model for the transformation of South Africa.

Mills was concerned about how workers like Laolang, residents, and tribal officials perceived the mine. He was troubled that the executive team resigned itself around either the view that *this is Africa* or a cynical justification: *the last one standing wins.*

He feared that some of the unions, including Laolang's, were going to take hard-line positions in upcoming negotiations.

Mills's strategy was to launch several change efforts at the same time. He introduced powerful management programs such as Six Sigma and Enterprise Resource Planning (ERP). He restructured, and he implemented DuPont's safety technology. He also brought in consultants whom he had worked with in the past to assess what could be done to transform a complex agenda of issues.

The problems were so vast that other CEOs might have quit on the spot. There were not only silos, the consultants told executives in 2004, but also subsilos. Almost no one thought from an overall vision for Lonmin. Short-term business outcomes were in trouble. Leadership processes were missing. Teams and communication structures lacked rigor and consistency, worsened by the fact that workers spoke six different languages. Community issues were, as the university study indicated, a ticking time bomb. Costs were rising, safety was declining (sixteen people had died in the Lonmin mines the year before), absenteeism was rising, and the communities were strangling with 40 percent unemployment and the HIV epidemic.

Mills's situation was dire, if not impossible. As he told us, "If we didn't move on all fronts, the community wouldn't tolerate us anymore." Mills had promised the financial markets (Lonmin is publicly traded in London) that the situation would turn around, and the analysts and investors were watching intently. "We had to do it all at once," he said, "even though most people said we couldn't."

Mills, Laolong, and all of Lonmin were on a collision course with the *default future*—the future that was going to happen unless something dramatic and unexpected happened. The default future is a function of how situations occur to all of the people involved. Unless the occurring could shift for thousands of people, the odds were stacked against Lonmin. As most management efforts do not consider how situations occur, most of them don't work—73 percent of change efforts fail,[1] and 70 percent of new strategies fall short of expectation.[2] The default future is too strong a force to be undone by good intentions, sophisticated systems, or new management efforts.

You might take a moment and reflect on situations in your work and life that aren't working. They are probably not as dramatic as Mills's, but they may be as problematic. Is there something that is pressing in on you or your organization, something that requires an urgent response?

Think about the performance challenge you identified. Does it keep recurring? Do you or others feel stuck? Notice that your future, like Lonmin's, is already written. It is an essential part of how situations occur to you and others. Unless you can alter how those situations occur, the default future is speeding toward you.

The Need for Something New

Michael Jensen, Barbados Group member and Harvard Business School professor emeritus, suggests that business needs new models that do a better job of predicting how people perform. Current models say that people behave in accordance with their mental assets—skills, intelligence, emotions, beliefs, values, attitudes, and knowledge. It's no wonder that the development of people in an organization is relegated to the training department and takes a backseat to process improvement.

If Mills were to follow a traditional development approach, he would work to ensure that Laolang (and his twenty-five thousand fellow workers) had appropriate incentives and skills training. Posters with catchy slogans would hang everywhere.

Mills, in short, would make every effort to motivate and train Laolang until his and his colleagues' behavior changed.

Given the reality of Laolang's mind-set and that of his fellow employees, these approaches would have failed. Not only would they not have achieved desired results, but they also would have become more evidence for the workers of why management is manipulative and thinks of employees only as tools.

After assessing the odds, Mills decided that making a series of changes in a consecutive and linear way would not succeed, and that his best bet was to transform everything at once—to rewrite the future of the company and all of its leaders, its employees, and the residents in the local communities.

For Laolang and many other workers, the most important issue was that the company occurred as hostile, filled with a few people who had all the power and thought of them only as tools.

Notice the reality illusion at work. As long as situations occurred this way to the workers of Lonmin, their actions would be defensive and passively resistant at best, defiant and homicidal at worst. Taken together, their actions would produce poor performance. Whether people liked it or not, that was their future.

No amount of training, skills acquisition, or motivational posters will change how the situation occurs. In fact, each of these "solutions" simply becomes more evidence for Laolang that the world is as he sees it. The same is true for each of us.

Other Impossible Situations

Lonmin is such an extreme case that it's easy to say it's not relevant to the rest of us. To see the universality of the First Law, we'll turn to Northrop Grumman's aerospace operation in Southern California in 2001. Although a very different world from the one of Lonmin in South Africa, similar dynamics were at play. At Northrop Grumman, scientists, engineers, and senior managers were facing a very different set of cir-cumstances but, as it occurred to them, a similarly challenging situation. To continue its growth the company needed to enter new markets, such as reusable launch vehicles and space exploration systems. But the company's contemporary track record and expertise were in delivering technology for defense programs, such as bomber and fighter aircraft. The last major human space flight contract had been the Apollo lunar module in the 1960s. How were the executives with this commitment going to get people on board for a plan requiring a shift in skills and technologies, especially when they had no guaran-tees it would work? The First Law tells us that, at the very least, you have to alter the way that market opportunity occurs to people. If it occurs as far-fetched, people's actions will be detached, cautious, perhaps cynical and resigned. If the market opportunity occurs as doable, important, worthwhile, people will put in the extra effort.

At Northrop Grumman, seventy people, using the ideas in this book, shifted how this market opportunity occurred to them, and then somehow transferred this shift to the entire workforce. As this happened, people's performance shifted, and Northrop Grumman is now considered a viable NASA human space flight prime contractor.

Now consider another example, one in South America. Petrobras, Brazil's state-run oil company, is one of the largest in the world. At the end of 1997, the oil monopoly ended in Brazil, challenging Petrobras to become competitive in the open market, which led Petrobras to create a Business Transformation Agenda. As part of the response, the company launched an Enterprise Resource Planning process to replace most of its more than one thousand systems.

A highly qualified team of more than 650 people from Petrobras and consulting firms came together to work on this project, making it the largest and most complex such ERP implementation in the world at that time. This project was named Sinergia, and its motto was "We are building a new success story for Petrobras."

As the project evolved, the team faced many complex challenges. At the end of 2001, right before the first "go live" implementation, the Brazilian government radically changed its oil and gas tax regulations, raising a major new hurdle in the system. The initial "go live" date had to be pushed back for four months. Tension, discomfort, and miscommunication among teams and executives began to plague the project.

In this environment, past issues between external consultants and Petrobras team members started to get out of hand, affecting both productivity and the climate of the group. People became skeptical about whether the initiative could succeed by the new scheduled date. There was also a lot at stake for the professionals involved in the project. At one point, conflict arose among the project consultants, executives, and managers, negatively affecting the team's performance to move forward.

The First Law explains why they were stuck. The implementation began to occur to people as futile—and somewhat threatening. People's actions correlated with how the situation occurred, and team conversations stalled.

In response to the pressure to make something happen, the team's manager, Jorge Mattos, decided to bring in Steve's company, now called the Vanto Group. Mattos realized that a critical success factor was missing: alignment around key commitments. Steve's colleagues began with a program for the eighty top leaders of the company. In the course of three and a half days, Mattos and the managers were able to leave behind past issues and conflicts, focusing the team on the same picture.

Mattos reflected back on this time in an interview with us recently. "We had a lot in our way," he said. "Not just the pressures on us, but how we did things in the past that were no longer working well. We needed to get a new view of ourselves and what was possible. The way in which we looked at the project actually shifted, and when it did, excitement and energy took over the group. It was truly a good surprise—people didn't look the same when we left the program." As a team, they committed to the success of the group, not only their own set of goals to be accomplished. They came up with a timeline and a new set of commitments for the new "go live" date, all of which the team could not have accomplished in the previous year. The shift started when the situation went from occurring as almost impossible to occurring as doable. As the First Law points out, when occurrence shifts, actions do as well. The team successfully met the new "go live" target of July 1, 2002.

Before we return to Lonmin, let's consider your performance challenge in more detail. How does the situation occur to you? How does it occur to other people?

What, if anything, have you tried to do to change the situation? Where has change worked? Where has it failed? Did any of these efforts alter how the situation occurred to you and to the other people involved?

As counterintuitive as it may seem, most change efforts end up *reinforcing* how a situation occurs. Think about someone trying to lose weight. To the person, his weight occurs as *a problem I can fix*. He looks for a solution to his problem, like a diet; he goes on it and falls off it. Now his weight occurs as *a problem that requires more willpower than I have*. Because his actions will correlate to this occurring, he gives up, resigned that his weight is here to stay.

Most companies are locked in the same cycle: they are resisting a problem by trying to fix it, but the more they push, the more the problem pushes back. Companies often try to trim costs by tracking and cutting expenses. If done in a mode of command and control, management will occur to its employees as *untrusting and uncaring*. As a natural response, the employees hold back. The situation grows more frustrating as employees end up putting in less effort, making the financial situation worse.

The principle at work here is: *whatever you resist, persists*. If you can see any way that you are resisting your performance challenge, you'll see that you may be strengthening its hold on you and others—the more you have fought it, the stronger it became.

We'll get to what to do about the situation in Chapters Two and Three, but a big part of the answer is to notice that what is holding you in place is how the situation occurs, and by trying to change it, you may achieve the opposite of what you intend.

Taking It to the Community

Back at Lonmin, Mills's challenge was to create the kind of transformations that had happened at Northrop Grumman and Petrobras, but on a scale that had never been attempted before. He saw that the benefits of confronting the default future were worth a risk. The key was to shift how the situation occurred for the stakeholders, but in a very rapid fashion. With advice from consultants trained in the Three Laws, he decided to invite people critical to the success of the Lonmin turnaround to an initial meeting, regardless of their animosity or adversarial nature. Mills and his team invited one hundred leaders from the company, tribes, unions, and the community to a two-day meeting.

Mills decided to hold the meeting where most of the stakeholders lived, in the community of Wonderkop, a sprawling shantytown with dirt streets, dotted with mine workers' hostels. His advisors strongly disagreed, fearing for their personal safety and his. As many residents of the community told us later, "The white executives have never come here."

People from every segment of the company and community showed up. Some representatives from the unions came in miner's clothes, others in traditional African dress. Some locals were in blue jeans, others were adorned in their best but well-worn finery. Executives in casual business clothes arrived in a bus, afraid to drive their cars into the community. Wealthy and influential people drove up in expensive cars and walked the few steps of gravel driveway in spotless suits. Others arrived sweaty after walking miles to make this meeting. "There were times when we didn't know what was happening," Mills said later. "I'd never seen anything like it."

The local nightclub was the only facility in Wonderkop large enough for the meeting. Lonmin employees had papered over the disco lights, hung curtains over the bar, and set up a screen for a computer display. Power cords snaked across the ground to power the laptops and projectors. They cleaned up the bathrooms and brought in an air conditioner that failed within the first hour. Under the African summer sun, the room was quickly over 100 degrees.

Mills introduced himself as the new CEO of Lonmin. "I know there's a lot that's broken—and I want to listen to that, so we can fix it together," he said boldly, while also stuttering with excitement. "But I'm really here as someone committed to your success, the mine's success, and the well-being of families and communities. A long time ago, I realized that I wanted to play in a game so big that it would involve making a contribution that would go beyond my lifetime."

He continued, "I invited you to these two days to explore together what we could create if we all worked together in a new way. Obviously I'm American, working for a London company, and I'm not aware of all the difficulties you've had to deal with, but I have read extensively about it. But I do know that we share one thing in common: our humanity. If we work together as human beings, we can work together to create something very exciting."

He said that prior to Lonmin he had worked for companies that had made a difference for the people in the communities, as the company also became more successful. He then said that, based on his prior experience, the first task was for people to listen and to learn about each other's worlds. Once that was done people could see if they were committed to creating something new.

He then asked, "What is it you want me to know that's not working?"

People brought up overcrowding, AIDS, unemployment, violence, unsafe streets due to lack of lighting, union anger at other unions, and how management doesn't care about the workers.

One man walked forward to the microphone and said, "Brad, you know what would show us that you're serious? Sleep in a hostel with twelve mine workers, so you know what it's like for us."

Mills said, without a second of delay, "I promise you I'll do that," and wrote his promise on the flip chart, the sound of his writing echoing in the room. When he put the pen down, the walls of the nightclub shook with the applause from the crowd, although many in the room told us later they were certain he wouldn't really do it. "No CEO had ever been here before, and no one would sleep here," one attendee told us later.

That night, Lonmin hosted a dinner and party. As the participants danced and drank, several white executives said, "I never knew how bad it is here," their eyes darting to run-down buildings with little light in the streets.

The second day began with people acknowledging Mills and Lonmin for demonstrating a new level of willingness to deal with what wasn't working (including the same broken air conditioner). A gray-haired African woman, a resident of the community, said, "I really can't believe that you're here, and that you're actually listening to us." One of the white union representatives said, "I'm starting to realize that there may be some way we can work together." One tall Londoner, a corporate executive, shaking with emotion, said, "I realize I was living in a cocoon, unaware of what was going on here . . . and I'm committing to making this different in the future."

When emotions settled down, Mills brought up the next question: "What will happen if we don't find a new way to work together?" And the next: "How can we know what that future might hold?" If nothing changes, then the future will resemble the past. He started by recounting the previous year's statistics: "Sixteen people died last year in the mines . . . so maybe we'll get a little better and only fourteen will die . . . but there will be more deaths than we want."

Another speaker said, "And seventy people will probably die of AIDS."

Others jumped in: "There will be a strike." "There will be robbing and murders in the street." "The smelter will blow up again"—referring to the explosion shortly before the meeting that drove the stock price down. One of the executives declared, "Based on our increasing expenses, the company will go out of business in five to seven years." One woman said, "My son will finish school and have no job." All of these comments, and those that followed, were written on the giant projector screen, making the future that they all saw coming very real.

People nodded their agreement that the descriptions accurately captured what would happen if nothing changed. They had identified the default future.

The conversation shifted, at first slowly, even laboriously, to a declaration of a new future. One man tried to alter the conversation toward dealing with his complaints about the company, but another man shot back, "You have to get off it. Don't sabotage this!" At some point, everything predictable—the good, the bad, and the ugly—was up on the screen. The room quieted. There was no more to say.

At this point, the next step could be taken. The discussion turned to a question that filled the projector screen: "What are the opportunities that can be seized if Lonmin, the communities, and the unions commit to new powerful ways of working together?" People walked to the microphones and said, in turn: "One hundred percent literacy." "Full employment." "AIDS-free community." "Lonmin is recognized and is successful on the world stage." The mood shift in the room was palpable, going from sober to excited, from imprisoned to free.

Partway through the process, one of the participants shouted, "This future is worth creating—how do we do it?" Mills took the microphone. "First, this process is going to take many years, and will require long-term commitment from each and every one in the room—and others not involved yet. Second, a series of initiatives could start in about two months, including a leadership program for all key stakehold- ers. Third, a process this complex—to transform a company of twenty-five thousand employees and communities of three hundred thousand people—would require solving problems no one has even identified yet, and the only element that could take the group through those obstacles would be your ongoing commitment."

Mills ended the meeting by saying,

> I'm committing myself and my organization to fulfilling this future that we've begun to articulate. I can't do it by myself, and my organization can't do it by itself, so we need you to match our commitment. If you are committed to creating this future, with others and me, there will be large sheets of paper on the wall by the door. At the top of the sheet it says, "I'm committing myself to creating a new future for Lonmin and our communities." Sign your name on that sheet.

After he thanked them for attending and participating, the meeting ended. All but two attendees signed their names on those sheets, with some putting down an "X" because they didn't write. (The two who didn't sign ended up joining and participating in the initiatives that followed.)

Mills told us later: "I wasn't sure if there would be any willingness for the process, but they were seriously on board. We were blown away!"

Chris Ahrends, an Anglican priest who for many years as the CEO of the Desmond Tutu Peace Centre, attended the session. After the meeting, he said to Brad and the consulting team, "If you can do 10 percent of what you're talking about, it will be revolutionary."

The Night in the Hostel

Several weeks later, Mills and another executive again overrode his advisors' objections and slept in the hostel, alongside the workers. When he woke up the next morning, it was to the sight of African warriors guarding him. "I wasn't just safe, I was the safest man in South Africa," he remarked to us. At 4:00 AM, to demonstrate his resolve, he and the regional coordinator for the National Union of Mineworkers, Victor Tseka, went to greet the workers arriving for their shift. Mills said later, "People couldn't believe I was the CEO. One of the workers went to the office and pulled out a copy of a company brochure with my picture before some of the men would believe us."

For Mills, the act of sleeping in a hostel was simple and powerful—in his words, "no big deal." But Mills understood the power of symbols to shift how situations occurred to people, challenging the default future and bringing about new levels of performance. For the workers, his actions sent a message so strong it's hard to capture in the pages of a book. "We couldn't believe it," one union representative said, "and we began to think we could actually trust this man." Laolang said, "Mills gained so much trust that people were willing to try it his way and see if it could work."

From the perspective of the First Law, Mills's actions make a lot of sense. He knew that, before he even started, he occurred to the workers as a typical CEO—viewing employees as tools, not caring about their welfare, and out only for money. People's sense of the default future was that he would make promises and then exploit the workers. His management plans, he knew, occurred as management mumbo jumbo. At worst, the initiatives would ask them for more effort with nothing in exchange. If he didn't shift how these situations occurred—and fast—nothing he did would make any impact. The default future would have come to pass.

The meeting in the nightclub was designed to shift how the executives, and the program they advocated, occurred to stakeholders. Mills made progress in this regard by listening so intently that people knew he heard them, that he saw their issues from their perspective. As people saw him listening—really listening—how he occurred to them began to shift from an arrogant CEO to a person who at least cared enough to spend a day with them. How Lonmin occurred altered from a company that was only out for profits to an advocate for the community. When Mills spent a night in the hostel and welcomed workers at the 4:00 AM shift, he occurred to them as a fellow human being.

With Mills, his fellow executives, and the management initiatives now occurring in a different way, people's behaviors shifted from resistant and angry to open and even somewhat receptive. He was now ready to begin the next phase of programs, which became known as the March Initiatives, when the heavy lifting of elevating performance began to take place.

Using Conversation to Shift Action

The March Lonmin Initiatives sought to shift action by transforming how the company occurred to about 150 people at a time, totaling 15,000 people over four years. This program used a systematic series of conversations among the program leaders, Lonmin executives, and the participants. People got to know each other in new ways that went beyond stereotypes, prejudices, and past conversations. Because performance matches how a situation occurs, this shift made an immediate and tangible difference in people's actions. At the same time, people explored and evaluated the default future. Not liking what it foretold, they rewrote the future, leading to the beginning of a stunning organizational transformation.

In addition to the conversations between the two women described at the start of this chapter, two specific incidents illustrate why Laolang, and hundreds of other people, were so moved by the process.

The first incident happened on the second day of the program, when people broke into groups representing each of the unions as well as management. Following the guidance of the program leaders, each identified the "games they play" in negotiating with the other groups. Management owned up to playing the "take it or leave it" card, crying poverty, using veiled threats, and reporting data selectively. Laolang's union acknowledged that it organized sit-ins, used wildcat strikes, burned property, and didn't tell management what it really thought because, in their words, "we don't trust them." As people described and admitted playing these games to the entire group, they started to laugh—both at themselves and, as they told us later, at the absurdity of playing games like this at all. They saw the default future, and they found it ridiculous.

As people reported their negotiation games, people saw the other side as more like themselves than they would have thought possible just a day before. More important, how unions occurred to management, and management to unions, began to shift—from opponents playing hardball to fellow human beings who shared the same virtues and weaknesses. People began to experience their old adversaries as allies, on the same side, committed to building a new future together.

The second incident happened later that day. The facilitators posed the question, "What are you committed to in future negotiations?" After hours of debate, much of it passionate, the hundred people who had come into the room a few days before as enemies left the room committed to more than a dozen points, including

- Total transparency—full disclosure—total information
- Respect for each other
- Creating a future that is the context for problem-solving bargaining
- Engaging each other with integrity

Each of the incidents described shows the shift in how the situations occurred to the people in the room. With alterations to this occurring, individuals who had been adversaries were able to work together on setting joint commitments—the seed of building something new. As dozens of people told us in interviews after the fact, this level of cooperation was possible only because how people saw the situations, each other, and the company had shifted. Once situations occurred in new ways, people moved beyond mere compliance to accountability, from merely doing their jobs to providing leadership. As the First Law asserts, people's performance and how the situations occur *always* match up. As people began to create a new vision, their actions automatically fell in line with what they were creating.

Transformation: Beyond Change Management

Notice that although Laolong didn't change a few things—his attitude, work ethic, and negotiation style—it's as though he became a new person. What we noticed most of all is that the angry man who saw nothing but fighting in his future was replaced by a man who appeared to be at peace and couldn't stop smiling.

He talked about managers and executives (no matter their race or backgrounds) as being real people—not as the caricatures of evil and manipulation they had seemed to him before. He promised to become an advocate for the commitments from the Lonmin leadership initiatives, and he was true to his word. Most remarkable is that the same shift happened to all of the fifteen thousand people who attended the leadership program.

We asked how it all occurred to Laolang. He told us:

> It was like a different South Africa after the program. Nelson Mandela started talking about the transformation of South Africa when he got out of prison, and became president. I had no idea what he really meant, but now I see the possibility of changing the world itself, beyond a single company like Lonmin. It created a very big space with me. This approach to transformation is everything. I understood very clearly that it takes individuals to put themselves in that space of committing. I take that as a rescue process for everyone in Lonmin and beyond.

The Future Rewritten

Besides a stronger, more collaborative culture in the company, a powerful sense of alignment for building a future has expanded. The company and community have developed a powerful framework and projects to forward sustainability.

The real accomplishment has been altering how situations occur to thousands of people, and as this has happened, their performance has shifted accordingly. Productivity reached one-million-plus platinum ounces in concentrate for the first time in its history. Lost-time injuries have decreased by approximately 43 percent, a reduction that continues to be sustained and improves over time. For the first time, the community is actively supporting the company. Not only are people creating something new, but also the evidence demonstrates that they achieve it. As Mills stepped down from the CEO role in 2008, he reflected on the events of the last several years. He told us, "In my mind, we succeeded on all fronts. I know we made a huge difference and this transformation will live on through the people it touched."

On the week of his seventy-fifth birthday, Nobel Peace Prize winner Desmond Tutu visited Lonmin. In talking about the company and its efforts to rewrite the future of everyone it touches, he said, "I have put my reputation, my name, on the line, to say to you here that I believe these people. I have a sense of their integrity."

Soon thereafter, the World Bank's International Finance Corporation (IFC) invested $100 million to help realize the dream of a self-sufficient Greater Lonmin Community.

If Lonmin and the three hundred thousand people who live in the surrounding community can alter how they occur for each other, this effort may become a model of organizational transformation.

What about you? There are specific actions you can take to tap into the power of the First Law of Performance. Notice the connection between performance and how situations occur for people. See that this relationship *always* holds.

See the reality illusion at work, in you and people around you. Almost without exception, people don't notice that all they are aware of is how situations occur to them. They talk, and act, as if they see things as they really are.

Find people whose actions make no sense to you. Ask them questions, mostly open-ended, that provide insight into how those situations are occurring to them. Keep going until you can see how their actions perfectly fit how the situation occurs to them. (You'll often find that this process alone goes a long way toward developing trust and cooperation.)

Become aware of how your own performance correlates with how situations occur to you.

- Notice that attempts to change a situation often backfire—strengthening, rather than altering, how the situation occurs. Remember: whatever you resist, persists.

- Consider: What if you could do something about how situations occur—to you and everyone around you? What impact would this make in everyone's performance?

In the next chapter, we'll explore the Second Law, which shows the inner workings of occurrence.

Where Is the Key
to Performance?

An old man was walking home late one night when he saw a friend on his knees under a street light, searching for something. "What are you doing?" he asked his friend.

"I dropped the key to my house."

"I'll help you look." After a few minutes of frustrated searching, the old man asked, "Where exactly were you when you dropped this key?"

His friend pointed toward the darkness. "Over there."

"Then why are you looking for it here?"

"Because this is where the light is."

This Sufi parable illustrates something that is all too common in companies and personal lives: many of us search for, but can't ever seem to find, the key to performance.

The search itself makes sense. Performance is what matters, and that comes down to actions taken by individuals. Unless people's actions shift, new strategies will fail, merger and acquisition goals will go unrealized, and new technologies won't deliver on their goals. On the personal side, unless we alter our actions, we'll never keep our New Year's resolution, improve our family life, or enhance our finances.

Consider that this description is accurate. Despite the billions that companies spend to refine strategies, redo reporting relationships, acquire companies, or be acquired—nevertheless, performance gains, which are usually the whole point, remain just out of reach. Without performance elevation, most efforts eventually fail.

How is it that, with all we know in the twenty-first century, performance gains aren't more forthcoming?

Consider that we're searching for the key to performance in the illumination provided by *knowledge*. If we have a problem, we check to see whether we know a solution, and if we don't, we go to people who are experts and ask them—by hiring consultants, reading books, or searching web sites. But as Jeffrey Pfeffer showed in *The Knowing-Doing Gap*, more information often doesn't translate into different action. We are searching for the key to performance in places it's easy to look for, rather than in the dark, unfamiliar, hidden places.

This chapter picks up where Chapter One left off. If we can shift how a situation occurs, new action will follow. Enough new actions from enough people will move the needle on performance. The key to performance, we assert, lies in the complex workings of occurrence—and that is the focus of this chapter.

Once found, the key to performance will allow you to alter your actions, and work with others to alter theirs, to take performance to a new level.

In this chapter, it's useful to think of a performance challenge that you or others are facing—either the same one you used in the last chapter or a new one. We'll move through cases and discussions, stopping along the way to consider your challenge in light of this material.

Searching for the Key to Performance at the Polus Group

The story of the Polus Group shows a company that hit a performance challenge, and how they found the key to turning the situation around.

In the aftermath of World War II, Toshimi Nakauchi's business education started when he and his wife sold bananas on the streets of Tokyo. "Bananas are one of the staples," his widow told us in 2007, "and that's what he was looking for—something people would always want." Reflecting back on those times, including raising three young children, his widow told us, "It was really hard." Smiling, she said, "I would put Kojiro [her middle son] inside a box of bananas to sleep during business hours."

Nakauchi's entrepreneurial interests pulled him toward real estate. Eventually he told one of his suppliers that he was planning to move on. The man tried to talk him out of his decision. "How much do you want to earn?" was the supplier's question to Nakauchi. "Ten thousand yen per day" was his answer, an outrageous number that was four times as much as the owner of the banana company was receiving.

Time proved that Nakauchi wasn't merely wishing. He became so successful that he built his own house, even adding a second floor for his office. He read, he studied, he questioned, and he demonstrated a knack for investing in land that quickly appreciated in value. He added to this investment strategy by building houses on his land and attracting talented colleagues; within a few years he was looking at a massively expanding business.

His search for good land values led to the village of Koshigaya, where, hundreds of years earlier, travelers would rest on their way to a mountaintop Shinto holy place called Nikko, the burial site of a famous shogun. Today, Koshigaya is a town of light industry and homes, known for its "Daruma dolls," which symbolize strong determinism and good fortune while memorializing the spread of Buddhism from India to China.

He imagined the day when he and his colleagues would be at the center of the housing industry around which the rest of the industry would rotate, much as Confucius considered the North Star (Polaris) to be for the heavens. In July 1969, he named the company the Polus Group to capture this vision.

From One Man's Vision to a Crisis of Continuity

As a man of vision, Nakauchi designed his company to become a large conglomerate from the beginning. For example, when the Polus Group employed just twenty people, he brought in a personnel specialist from the government to teach the executives how to organize human resources for growth. The expert was trained by the U.S. Army during the occupation of Japan and later was in charge of setting up the personnel systems at Honda.

Houses designed by the Polus Group have a signature look—modern and multifaceted, many with porches. Their large windows and light woods are warm and inviting, resembling upscale developments in beach communities in the United States.

The president took special care to forge personal relationships with employees, joking that he was able to remember everyone's name only up through the one-thousandth hire. He emphasized education, believing that "top crest" individuals had a key message that could build the capacity of the company's staff. He brought in management thinkers, artists, even a famous Olympic volleyball coach, to lecture to employees. The founder asked each speaker to record the essence of their message in Japanese calligraphy. Today, these framed documents hang around the Polus Group's conference rooms and offices.

As the Polus Group grew to become the large conglomerate it is today, his three sons took positions as managers in the growing firm. Nakauchi's leadership combined vision, operational excellence, and strong relationships.

In 1999, the founder suffered an incapacitating stroke. The leadership void in the Polus Group was unexpected and devastating. One senior manager told us: "We had a visionary leading our work and then, all of a sudden, we didn't know what to do." Homma, the head of human resources, said, "We lost our future."

Nakauchi's incapacitation caused people both inside the Polus Group and outside to wonder if the family-owned company could continue to grow, or would even survive. Could his three sons provide the leadership, relationship, vision, and experience that their father had?

Despite their personal sadness and grief, they made one good-faith effort after another to move ahead without their leader—discussing reorganizations, new roles, different strategies.

The company had a lot of talent to draw on. Each of the president's sons seems to have one of his gifts. The oldest,

Keitaro, is a visionary leader. Kojiro, the middle brother, targets operational excellence. Akio, the youngest, focuses on relationships.

Still, nothing seemed to work. Several people told us, "We kept spinning through the same issues, over and over." It was conversation without end, argument without resolution.

In their words, they were "sinking into confusion," had "no charisma in the group," were "stagnating," with "no energy," "tired," and "muddled." Their most common word was "stuck."

If the individuals had been bound in ropes, they would have found a way to untie them or cut them loose. Unfortunately, the ties that held them were not so obvious. As people told us, "We didn't know what was holding us back."

What was holding them back was outside the boundaries of where they were looking—in the dark, not in the light of their knowledge.

The Second Law of Performance

How a situation occurs arises in language.

"Business as usual" explanations of the Polus Group's situation would focus on succession planning, strategy, or roles and responsibilities. But consider that something much deeper was at work. As we will see, these deeper issues are likely at work in your performance challenge as well.

As counterintuitive as it may seem, the people in the company were tied up in knots of language—knots composed of words, symbols, sentences, and communication that somehow had blocked and impeded performance. The result was repetitive and unproductive behavior, mostly done with the best of intentions.

How situations occur is inseparable from language. We know of no bolder illustration of this fact than the case of Helen Keller, who had learned only a few words before she lost her sight and hearing to an illness when she was eighteen months old. Seven years later, she learned sign language through her tutor, Anne Sullivan. Keller describes her life before meeting Sullivan, and the moment when she learned language:

> For nearly six years I had no concepts whatever of nature or mind or death or God. I literally thought with my body. Without a single exception my memories of that time are tactual. I was impelled like an animal to seek food and warmth. I remember crying, but not the grief that caused the tears.... I was like an unconscious clod of earth. Then, suddenly, I knew not how or where or when, my brain felt the impact of another mind, and I awoke to language, to knowledge of love, to the usual concepts of nature, of good and evil! I was actually lifted from nothingness to human life.[3]

How the world occurred to Keller, once she learned language, shifted more dramatically than most of us can imagine. Notice that language wasn't something she understood bit by bit as her teacher taught her various signs. Language grabbed her, reshaping every part of her awareness in a moment of awakening. She captured the experience when she wrote that before the moment she "knew only darkness and stillness ... my life was without past or future ... but a little word from the fingers of another fell into my hand that clutched at emptiness, and my heart leaped to the rapture of living."[4]

After learning language, the past and future appeared to her, like television screens turning on for the first time. For the rest of her life, Keller drew audiences for her lectures and readers for her books, as much for the uniqueness of her outlook as for the drama of her life's story. She saw language for what it is: a force that makes us human, that gives us a past and a future, that allows us to dream, to plan, to set and realize goals.

Most of us are too young when we begin to acquire language to recall that moment for ourselves. It seems that language has always been with us, like breathing. We don't pay attention to its presence.

But consider: Language is the means through which your future is already written. It is also the means through which it can be rewritten. For people at the Polus Group, and all of us, there's good news in this insight.

The people at the Polus Group couldn't change the fact of the president's incapacitation. In our lives there are facets that are beyond our control. In fact, consider your performance challenge. Your boss, your finances, your children, your industry, your country—are all resistant to change. (Did your parents try to change you? How well did that go?) But as the First Law of Performance says, your actions correlate with how these *occur* to you, not to the facts themselves.

The key to performance is hiding in a particular facet of language that we'll get to in the next section. First, we have to map the connections of language and occurrence.

The Knots of Language

Language is used here in the broadest sense. It includes not only spoken and written communication, but also body language, facial expressions, tone of voice, pictures and drawings, music, how people dress, and any other actions that have symbolic intent.

Untying the knots of language begins with seeing that whenever you say something, other communication is carried along with it. We call this phenomenon *the unsaid but communicated*. Sometimes the sender is aware of the unsaid; often they are not. The unsaid is the most important part of language when it comes to elevating performance.

The unsaid but communicated includes (but is not limited to) assumptions, expectations, disappointments, resentments, regrets, interpretations, significance, and issues that occur as dangerous.

We all know what it's like to talk to someone who is hiding something. He often appears as evasive, detached, distant, or disconnected. What he's hiding is in the unsaid, but the way he comes across communicates that something is off. Think of an entire group of coworkers hiding things from each other, and you'll see the impact the unsaid has on performance.

You can feel and experience the unsaid but communicated. Observe a family having dinner in a restaurant and you'll notice the way family members occur to each other. You may not be able to hear anything they are saying, but in watching you may see that one person broadcasts "How long is this going to last?" Another emits "It's great being together," and a third conveys "When are they going to get along? And I wonder if anybody notices."

When you walk into a company for a meeting, make a sales call, or apply for a job, you can see, instantly, how the company occurs to employees, and how people occur to each other. Like little cartoon bubbles floating over people's heads, you can read what people are not saying but are communicating. The messages run the gamut, from "I'm so bored and I wonder what's for lunch," to "My work is more important than yours." This communication is channeled in many different ways—in what people say, how they say it, their gestures, tones, eye contact, and so on. If you turn up your antennae to pick up the unsaid, it can be overwhelming. It seems to spring from the essence of who people are, and comes through in every encounter. Just to make it through the day, we often turn our antennae off.

Now we get to an aspect of communication that writes our future without our even realizing it. It is the part of language that exists outside the light of our attention.

We call this aspect that which is *unsaid and communicated without awareness*. It determines and shapes which messages are possible, not possible, important, unimportant, relevant, not relevant, appropriate, not appropriate, and so on. The unawareness aspect puts this part of language outside our control. Until we find leverage on this part of language, the future is written and can't be altered.

The Key to Performance

Altering what was unsaid and communicated without awareness was the key to turning around the Polus Group. The process starts with becoming aware of what people aren't saying but are communicating.

For most people, exploring the unsaid is like walking into a cave—the journey goes from bright to dim to pitch black. It starts with people saying what they have been thinking. After a time, the person will say something and feel surprised by what she has just said, as if another person uttered the words. The expression on her face shifts from remembering to exploring—as if she's discovering the terrain by touch. The further a person goes, the more she needs a guide who knows the terrain of the unsaid.

At the Polus Group, Keitaro felt bound and trapped by his situation, including his sudden ascent to power, his relative youth in the position, the loyalty that employees felt to the founder but not to him, and so on. It wasn't the actual situation that bound him; it's what he and others made the situation mean, through language—and didn't talk about.

In the confidences of one-on-one meetings, people were initially concerned about their answers, careful about what they said and didn't say.

Consultants helped people examine the unsaid. As the process continued, people went from disclosing what they thought but never said to discovering what was lurking behind their thoughts and opinions. When all was said and done, for each person, what they weren't saying was some variant of the same thing: *I'm doing the best I can but other people's agendas are keeping what I'm doing from working. If only the founder were here, he would fix it, but he's not, so all I can do is just keep trying.*

At the Polus Group, the unsaid, and especially the unsaid that people were unaware of, left people with *no space to create anything new.* They were resigned as a result of this knotted language that influenced and determined their behavior. They were bound, trapped, and had no room to design new ways of moving forward or fulfilling the opportunities of the business. This lack of freedom was a direct result of the unsaid that influenced how the situation occurred.

The *unsaid and communicated but without awareness* became linguistic clutter. The clutter was so widespread that people didn't have the freedom to create something new. We all know the feeling of trying to work at a desk that's cluttered with papers, folders, and sticky notes. There's no space in which to work. What's already there prevents anything new from happening. A closet with boxes and clothes that fall out when you open the door has no space for anything new. It can't be used for its purpose—storage—because it's already packed with stuff. You have to create a space, a clearing, and a sense that "nothing is in my way" so that you can put something new on the desk or in the closet.

Thinking about cluttered physical spaces gives us insights into what happens in situations in which people are bound by knots of language. Such situations occur as tiring, chaotic—things in the wrong place—and unfinished—letters on a desk screaming to be read, boxes in a closet demanding to be unpacked.

At the Polus Group, with the clutter squeezing out room to create, people rehashed old issues: roles and responsibilities, strategy, and what actions people should take. Without space, all that the Polus Group leaders could do was have another conversation, but they kept having the same discussion over and over—like in the movie *Groundhog Day*. The way it occurred to people was much like trying to push another box into an already full closet.

The key to performance isn't pushing new conversations about strategy or reorganization into an already crammed space; rather, it's clearing out the clutter.

Almost universally, it's the unsaid that's cluttered for individuals, groups, and organizations. Before anything new can happen, people need to make space by doing the linguistic equivalent of clearing out closets. This means moving issues into the light of discussion—saying them, examining them in public. The point here isn't to say every passing thought, or dump out every judgment or evaluation on everyone. It's certainly not to say every random thought that comes from your inner voice.

The point is to notice that there are issues constraining people because of what they aren't saying. When people can address and articulate the unsaid, space begins to open up. People can discuss—openly and in public—what's holding them back and what to do about it. Much like moving things out of the closet and into the room, people can sort through issues, perspectives, and grievances, with the intent of making more space.

Clearing Out the Closet

The oldest son, Keitaro, heard about Steve's previous work with organizations in Japan, and asked for proposals that would break the Polus Group's leadership stalemate. The consulting team began an initial process of discovery that resulted in a multistage plan, based on the Three Laws of Performance. The promise of the plan was to get the Polus Group unstuck.

Over dinner, Homma, the HR executive, put forward an idea so radical, it was almost unimaginable in Japan. Leaning forward, he said: "Steve-san, if we were to implement this plan of getting unstuck, we really need to start with *just* the family and board of directors."

Steve asked whether a foreigner would be allowed into so intimate a process.

Homma's response was, "We've always been a courageous company. If people think this is the way out of the trap we're in, I'm sure they'll take the risk."

The family and board of directors—eleven people—were about to embark on a unique journey made possible by the Three Laws of Performance. In particular, getting this small group unstuck required them to find and use the key to performance. We have the same goal for the readers of this chapter.

Our "Internal Voice"

To appreciate the journey of exploring the unsaid, we need to go back to our analogy of the cave. Imagine someone exploring in absolute darkness, going by touch alone. As he crawls, inch by inch, he's looking for recognizable objects: sudden drops, stalactites, water, and the like. If he finds a rough ridge growing from the floor up, he knows it's a stalagmite, and roughly how large it will be, and that he needs to crawl around it. His most valuable asset is his awareness of what sorts of things lurk in caves.

Likewise, as we move through the unsaid, there are forms and objects to look for. The first is the inner voice, which is the voice in your head that is constantly talking about everything and anything. You could consider it thinking, but it is really a conversation that you are having with yourself. Our internal voice runs so constantly that we mostly don't notice it. It has the quality of being like air to the bird or water to the fish—always present and never noticed.

Our internal voice is always asking and answering questions, such as: Is this true? Is this false? Is this right? Is this wrong? Is this good? Is this bad? What's the problem? What's the solution? What's the answer? What's the question? Why should I do this? How should I do this? Do I agree? Do I disagree? What's in it for me? What's in it for him or her or them?

In fact, if you take a moment right now and look at some of the commentary that you have been having with yourself about what you're reading, you'll hear your internal voice in action. The way this book occurs to you has a lot to do with the conversations you are bringing to it. This internal voice—the voice in your head that we're inviting you to listen to at this very moment—is talking to you so constantly that you can't turn it off even when you try.

In particular, think about your performance challenge, and notice what your internal voice has to say. For most people, it's something like *Maybe I'm not trying hard enough? Or I'm just plain unlucky? Will this book help? Probably not, but it would be nice if it did.*

Most of the time, the inner voice repeats old thoughts. Only rarely does it say anything new. And yet, it takes up a lot of our awareness. Notice that your inner voice probably won't produce any novel solutions to your performance challenge.

Rackets

As we continue our trek into the unsaid and continue the analogy of the cave, the interior grows darker. It's here that we find a form that most people aren't trained to spot. It's called a *racket*.

Becoming aware of rackets, and taking responsibility for them, is one of the most important aspects in elevating performance.

A racket has four elements. First, there is a complaint that has persisted for some time. *A common one in marriages: "He's late again!"* (Notice that "he's late again" swirls in the wife's internal voice.) Second, there is a pattern of behavior that goes along with the complaint. *The wife may act irritated, aloof, and withdrawn.* ("I'm really mad and disappointed" echoes in her internal voice.) People are generally aware of these first two elements.

Before moving on to the next two elements you might notice if your performance challenge has a racket associated with it. What's the complaint? Maybe *this isn't working.* Or *no one is giving me the help I need.* What's the pattern of behavior that goes with the complaint? Maybe it's *acting withdrawn,* or *snapping at people.* Notice that the complaint and the pattern of behavior are married. The complaint elicits the pattern of behavior, again and again. For some people, the pattern of behavior is so entrenched that others think *that's who he is.*

Continuing with our racket example, the third element is a payoff for having this complaint continue. The wife gets to be right, makes her husband wrong, avoids the domination of her husband (or what occurs to her as her husband's domination by being late), and lets her regain her control of the situation. The fourth element is the cost of this behavior. For every payoff, there's a cost. The cost here may be that the wife loses closeness with her husband, as well as intimacy, expression, satisfaction, and vitality. The last two pieces—the payoff and the cost—live in the *unsaid and unaware.*

What about the racket you identified? What's the payoff? Maybe *it helps me cope* or *I avoid the domination of this person/situation* or *I get to be right.* The payoff is what keeps the racket going, often for years.

What about the cost? Is it *self-expression? Joy? A feeling of being alive?* It was the cost of rackets, as we'll see, that was largely responsible for the Polus Group being tied up in knots.

People often ask, "Why is this called a racket?" Think back to the days of Prohibition in the United States and you'll see why. Some restaurants were fronts for illegal bars. The restaurant masqueraded as something other than what it really was: a cover for an illicit operation. The restaurant was a racket.

In our example, at first glance, it appears that the wife is upset at her husband for being late. In fact, she gets a payoff that may be worth far more than punctuality: she gets to be right and feel superior. She also has a card that will allow her to be late sometime in the future, as payback. What appears to be a legitimate complaint is actually a play for power.

As an aside, rackets inside of relationships are always perfectly paired. The husband here also has a racket of being late—whereby he gets to make his wife wrong for making him wrong. After all, "Why doesn't she appreciate how hard I'm working to keep us above water?"

The wife (and husband) running their "late again!" rackets are paying a price, about which they are both unaware. Yet the price is communicated in many conversations between them. For those who observe them, it is easily seen: *a lack of intimacy, a constant state of being withdrawn*, and *ongoing resentment*. It is unsaid and communicated, affecting the quality and experience of the relationship.

Think about your racket. Can you see how the complaint might be a disguise for something deeper, such as a way of controlling a situation, or avoiding the domination of another person?

Learning the Language

Our promise to you is that reading this book will lead to an ability to elevate performance. You can now see why. You'll have more power over a situation when you can label something a racket or can identify that what holds you back has something to do with how a situation occurs to you. It's not unlike a physician finding leverage over what holds people back from good health by correctly labeling an illness.

There's a reason people join communities when they make an in-depth study of something, like business or law. The support of others is important, and part of the study is learning to use a new language.

We suggest you make reading this book a group effort. Find others who are interested in elevating performance, and go through chapters with them. Discuss together your performance challenges and what you're learning from this book.

Whether you're reading alone or with others, we encourage you to join a community of readers on our web site, www.threelaws.com. You can post your insights, engage others in discussion, and contact both of us. Most important, you will enhance your ability to elevate performance.

Using the Second Law

At the Polus Group, many persistent complaints arose from what people believed were old agreements. Executives and family members told Steve's team about several agreements they had made:

- The brothers will work out individual differences in private.
- The oldest brother will run the company.
- The company will operate in three separate divisions, each run by a brother.
- Decisions require consent of the family.

The oldest brother would make decisions, and the others would object—thinking *we agreed that decisions require consent of the family*. The oldest brother would then shrug off the complaint, because of the agreement *to work out problems in private*. Their internal voices were filled with chatter about how the others weren't living up to what they said they would do.

It's important to note that many of these old agreements were never actually agreed to. Executives told Steve's team that the method of making decisions was ambiguous, while others insisted that these agreements were as real as anything on paper with signatures. Still, agreed to or not, they formed the basis of persistent complaints and took up much of the bandwidth in people's internal voices.

Although people in the situation are unaware of cost, an observer trained in the Three Laws can see it. Like a seasoned cave explorer, someone trained in the Three Laws knows a racket is at work when people act resigned and detached, not seeming to enjoy their work or each other's company, yet keeping up as good a front as they can. This was the case at the Polus Group. People looked isolated and resigned yet resolute that they would keep going on for the founder's sake.

Likewise, someone trained in the Three Laws can also see the payoff that people get for running their racket. After the founder's incapacitation, each of the brothers, and the board of directors as a whole, experienced the threat and risk of being unsure who would run the company and whether it would survive. Each of them was concerned about who would be in control and about not losing the control they already had. By running their rackets, they got to avoid the domination of each other and the situation itself. Although ineffective, this behavior occurred as the only option.

Everyone was trying their best, but the old agreements contradicted one another and tied the brothers and board of directors into knots. The oldest brother would make a decision, then the others would reject it. When no one made decisions, the executives looked to the family, which looked to the board, which looked back to the family. Throughout the process, people acted out rackets—fixed ways of behaving coupled with persistent complaints. Their internal voices were thick with objections, complaints, and words of despair. The net result was that the situation occurred as *no space to create anything new.*

Looking from your performance challenge, think about situations that hold you back, and you may be able to notice other rackets. Start with your internal voice and listen for complaints that have persisted for some time. Notice what you gain from having that complaint continue: probably something like being right, making others wrong, being justified, invalidating others, escaping from responsibility, and avoiding a dominating situation. Then begin to see the cost—it's usually some combination of love, health, happiness, and self-expression.

When we see the power of the unsaid, two compelling insights become clear. The first is that the situation is absurd. How the situation occurs to us is given by language, yet it occurs to people to be as real as a wall. You can bump into a wall, but you can't bump into the words that people reported were accurate descriptions of the Polus Group: "stuck," "difficult," "stressful," and "uncertain." Noticing that people were bound up in knots of language is, in itself, a freeing insight. We can untie the knots of language with different language.

The second insight leads to action: clear out the unsaid. Do this by saying what is unsaid and deal with it. At the Polus Group, discussing which agreements were real and which were imagined went a long way toward creating space. Getting the payoff and costs out into the open helped people discard some old conversations and make room for new conversations.

No matter how smart or insightful people are, we are all prone to being hijacked by what is unsaid—especially the unsaid about which people are unaware. Before moving more deeply into the Polus Group, we'll take a moment and examine how an understanding of the Second Law can dramatically shift a relationship between two people. This situation happened at the Harvard Business School.

The Harvard Business School: The Negotiation, Organizations, and Markets Unit

A group of six scholars in the Harvard Business School, led by Michael Jensen, had been researching and teaching new ideas about how firms, in many cases, actually destroy wealth. They were, in their own words, a group of rogue scholars. They were loyal and collegial with one another, having put their reputations on the line by joining the group. For example, Mal Salter, a senior professor at the Harvard Business School, was invited to join the group and did so because he was interested in mastering a new emerging subject field.

After some years of being the "renegades," the business school presented them with the opportunity to become a formal faculty unit, requiring them to establish a clear mission statement, a research agenda, and a program for attracting and developing new faculty. Jensen wanted the group to be more than a formality—he sought a culture of openness and respect, aligned around a common vision. He wanted it to be a genuine team, of the caliber rarely found in academia.

As Jensen said to us:

> We had been stuck in the mud, with complications of a renegade group that wasn't part of the organization for years. Now we were going to be an officially sanctioned group within the Harvard Business School. We were having a hard time "coming in from the cold." We weren't sure we wanted to be a sanctioned unit. We enjoyed being renegades and throwing intellectual hand grenades.

When the group met with Steve in July 1997, they listed many outcomes that would make their initial two days together surpass expectations. Most in the group, including a world-renowned psychologist, didn't think any of these goals could be achieved in a mere two days.

In the meeting, Steve asked people to list their persistent complaints about each other—beginning to probe the unsaid. Then he invited people to say what these were—*and move them into the realm of the said.* This would take some courage on their parts, opening up and saying what wasn't being said. After silence that seemed unending, Salter was the first to speak. He said that he and Jensen were friends and colleagues, and that he had immense respect for Jensen's work. He added, with a slight smile, that "Mike is sometimes headstrong and doesn't listen." He said it as though he was saying something that was descriptively true.

Steve pointed out that persistent complaints, by their very nature, aren't true descriptions of anything, although they are real as complaints. Here's what happened:

> Salter: What do you mean my complaints aren't
>   true? I love Michael, but he's headstrong
>   and doesn't listen; just ask anyone.
> Steve: Mal, that's a complaint you have about Michael, yes?
> Salter: Yes.
> Steve: The nature of a complaint is that some-
>   thing should not be the way that it is.
> Salter: Right, Michael should not be as head-
>   strong as he is, and he should listen.
> Steve: That's your complaint about Michael; it's not
>   Michael. It's actually a judgment about Michael.
> Salter: Yes, that's my judgment about Michael.

Steve: It's a real *complaint*, but it's not a real *description* of facts about Michael.

Salter: Oh ... [long pause] I don't know.

Given it was late in the day, Steve added, "Just think about it overnight, OK?"

The next morning, Salter walked in smiling at some insight he had developed. "I thought about our conversation all night," he said excitedly, "and you're right. It's just a persistent complaint! I realized there are times Michael has listened, obviously. And even when he doesn't, my complaining about it makes no difference. I get it."

Salter saw something of profound importance for performance. When something is lurking in the unsaid, it has the flavor—the occurrence—of being descriptively true. But it's nothing more than language—constructed and changeable.

Further, Salter saw that this bit of language in the unsaid was blinding him to behavior that contradicted it. In his mind, the fact was that Jensen was headstrong and didn't listen and, as a fact, left him working around the issue. Although Jensen and he continued to have a good working relationship, Salter knew it was less optimal than what was possible. As Salter told us years later, the team's productivity and learning had slowed down. What the Second Law reveals is that this slowdown—or as Jensen put it, a sense of "being stuck in the mud"—was a result of the unsaid at work—in this case, determining the way Jensen "was" for Salter. Further, Salter's conversations—with himself and with others—reinforced that "Michael is headstrong and doesn't listen." How Jensen occurred for Salter blinded him to behavior inconsistent with this label of the man. Through the act of moving the persistent complaint from the unsaid to the said, where it could be seen and discussed for what it was, his relationship with Jensen was elevated—or in Salter's words, "created clarity and openness of a new kind, accelerating the learning process in the team." Once he saw the complaint for what it was, Salter could build a stronger relationship with Jensen, in which he could make new requests to address his original concern. Salter elevated his ability to be an engaged partner in the relationship. All of this movement began with the linguistic equivalent of clearing out the closet.

In 2007, we interviewed Salter about what had happened all those years ago. He said: "The notion that behavior is a function of how the situation appears to be to the person ... to me, that cuts like a hot knife through butter." He added: "That's a big idea."

For years this group had been running away from being a formal faculty unit within the Harvard Business School. After this session, they were able, as a group, to make a commitment to a strategy of creating a new faculty unit. A month later they met and finished their work. The group was accepted as a unit within in the Harvard Business School, and over the years it has grown into one of the school's largest units.

Seeing this law at work has a dramatic impact on performance, as it begins to loosen the grip of absolute certainty that makes workplace conflict so entrenched. Once the people at Lonmin saw that their conclusions about other groups—management about the unions, each union about other unions, and so on—were lurking in the unsaid, allowing no space for listening, they were suddenly more able to listen. Even in cases in which people are already working effectively with others—like that of Professor Salter at the Harvard Business School—there is the possibility of accelerating and elevating their performance level by clearing out the unsaid. When people see the Second Law in action, they are often able to let go of their righteousness and take a big step toward collaboration. They can sort out the unsaid together, in public—discarding the bits that hold people back, and thereby opening up space. As we'll see in the next chapter, people can then fill the new space with a new vision that does what was impossible while people were stuck.

"I found this to be nothing short of incredible," Jensen told us. "With all the debris left on the road, we probably would have failed in the long run if we had not had this intervention."

You may notice your persistent complaints about situations and other people. Consider that they don't reside in reality, but in the unsaid of language, where they take on the occurrence of reality. (Remember the reality illusion.) Notice that as long as you take these persistent complaints to be true, you are "at the effect of them"—that is, your actions will be defensive, consistent with the way the situation occurs to you. By seeing that these gripes are the result of language at work, they become something you can impact—and we'll see a lot more about how to do this in the next chapter. Again, notice all four elements of a racket: the complaint, the pattern of behavior, the payoff, and the cost. For now, see the gears of the said and unsaid—language at work. More than a few people have reported that this insight starts a cascade of other insights that alters performance.

We now return to the Polus Group, where their journey to find and use the key to performance was about to begin. Like the Harvard Business School, they had issues in the unsaid that needed to be examined; but with so many people involved, the tangle of language and the solutions required were more complex.

As we move through this section, you might reflect on how this situation is like yours. What insights can you derive from this example that apply to your performance challenge?

Polus Group's Stage 0

The situation at the Polus Group was built on top of a web of personal dynamics, each strand of which was as powerful as what happened at the Harvard Business School. The risky program that Homma, the HR executive, described over dinner with Steve became known as "Stage 0," as it needed to happen before "Stage 1" that would involve all the senior managers.

Stage 0 began in the fall of 2001 with the four family members and seven other members of the board of directors. Beginning with a series of in-depth individual interviews with each of the participants, the entire group then went through a three-day process based on the Three Laws of Performance. The process allowed each person, and the group as a whole, to look into their individual and collective blind spots (the unsaid and unaware) in such a way that issues moved from the background to the foreground. The result, Steve promised, was that people would get unstuck and performance would make a major jump forward—even in areas where people felt resigned.

It's never easy in the early stages of this process for people to look into the dark and hidden aspects of the unsaid and articulate what is depriving them of space. It takes courage on the part of the participants and intentionality on the part of the facilitator.

Much of the first day was spent looking into the complaints people had. The most significant collective issue was people's regret over the loss of their leader. The theme of what people said was *if only he were here, we would know where to go next.* At the end of the first day no one was sure that anything significant would be accomplished. After all, they said, "These issues had been going on for years."

As often happens in this kind of process when people sleep on it overnight, things looked different the next day, as insights began to form that allowed people to articulate the unsaid. Others began to see that their view of the company and each other was colored by the loss of the founder and how they interpreted that situation. They began to see that they had taken as a given that the glory days of the company were over and they would never again be in a position of leading the industry. Because this was the way that it was and the way that it would be, all that was left to them would be learning to live with this new reality. Somehow, they would have to muddle through by doing the best they could in these "hard times." Until Stage 0, all of this was unsaid.

A critical point of this chapter is this: giving voice to the unsaid creates space. If the process went no further, this newfound room would allow people to choose a new direction for the company. Chapter Three shows how to take advantage of this new space to create something dramatically new.

Steve used several methods to explore the unsaid. In particular, he showed the structure of a racket and invited them to map this structure onto their situation.

As people said what their rackets were, the dynamic in the company shifted. The payoff of a racket works only because it operates below awareness. Disclosing a racket has the same effect you would get from hanging a sign that says "Alcohol Served Here" on the front of the Prohibition-era bar posing as a restaurant. The gig is up. The façade no longer works.

Example of a Group Racket

Racket: they aren't leading the way the old president did.

Fixed way of behaving: resigned, sad, isolated, and detached.

Payoffs:	Organizational Costs:
Making "us" right, making "them" wrong	Power
Self-justification of our group's avoiding the domination of "them"	Effectiveness
	Productivity
	Business viability
	Morale

People noticed that, with this group racket in place, the future of the Polus Group was already written.

Turning to your performance challenge, what would happen if you disclosed your racket to those it affects? The racket would lose its impact, just as happened in the Polus Group, and you would then need to address the underlying issues.

Most rackets begin with a complaint over which the person feels no sense of power. You might check to see if this was the case for you. If so, disclosing the racket will bring you back to that complaint and allow you to deal with it in a way that will give you a sense of power. We'll get to that part of the process in the next chapter.

Another of the methods that Steve and his team used to probe the unsaid was to have the family members and executives write a letter to the founder that expressed how his incapacitation impacted them. Steve asked them to include in their letter anything they needed to say, anything they needed to forgive or be forgiven for, anything they needed to take responsibility for, or anything they needed to give up. In doing so, people used language to probe their blind spots and move issues into actual discussion where the impact could be dissipated.

As people wrote their letters, some cried, others looked thoughtful, some smiled with the memories of his vision, hard work, and gentle style. When everyone had finished writing, people read their letters to the group. Part of Homma's letter says:

> It has been three years since you [the president] got sick and were taken away from the management of our company. While we've been trying to develop our power as a group, there were many times things didn't work as well as they could.
>
> I realize that in the background there's been grief and blame amongst ourselves and even with you, and now that I see this, I'm giving it up. I know that if you were here and able to tell me, you would want me to do that.
>
> I take these insights as an opportunity for our management to come together and create a new vision. We have many powerful managers here, and it's a shame we haven't stepped forward as you would want us to. I'm certain that we have greater power than what we have expressed so far and now that we have gotten ourselves out of our way. I commit to you and myself that I will be a front-runner for a new future.

Some letters expressed gratitude to Nakauchi, thanking him for the career opportunities they'd had. Others said they loved him and acknowledged that they had been hoping for his return. People recalled the framed calligraphy in the conference room, his respect among Japanese business and government leaders, his beginnings from selling bananas after World War II.

As people articulated what hadn't been said before, issues came forward that, until then, had been invisible. Participants began to test the idea that, while the facts of the founder's incapacitation were indisputable, the impact of that loss and what it meant to each of them arose in language. So although they couldn't do anything about the founder's health condition (the facts), they might be able to alter how the situation occurred to them. The writing of the letters went a long way toward probing the unsaid, giving them room to articulate something new.

Keitaro, the oldest son, had two insights as people read their letters. First, he realized that what he thought was showing respect to his father was actually holding people back. When we interviewed Keitaro later about the program, he said, "I thought I was showing responsibility to my brothers by insisting we follow my father's strategies. But I see now that I was actually depriving them of the opportunity to be leaders." Again, articulating the unsaid creates the room to say something new.

Second, Keitaro said that he never saw himself as an executive. "I was not a leader who could lead and coordinate people. I was primarily a keeper of my father's legacy."

After these bits of the unsaid were articulated, people were able to have conversations they couldn't have before. Keitaro announced that he was now stepping up as a leader and "a coordinator of people." He added, "I now am ready and want my brothers to be leaders with me." Akio quietly asserted that "I'm going to involve the community in new ways as my father would have done." Homma stood up, surveying the entire group, and proclaimed, "I can't figure out our future by myself—but I am going to put together the people and process for living up to, and going beyond, what our founder would have wanted."

From the perspective of the Second Law, how the situation occurred to the family and executives altered. It went from *If only he were here . . . we would know where to go next* to *We can go beyond what our founder intended.* This alteration in how the Polus Group occurred elicited new, elevated performance. People were no longer stuck.

Notice that these actions had a dual effect. Not only did they bring the unsaid into the said, and thus create space, but they also made the future less certain. It was as though, each step of the way, white paint was beginning to cover over an old painting. Soon there would be enough blank canvas on which to write a new future.

Rewriting the future begins with shifting how a person occurs to himself. Think of Laolong in Chapter One, the three brothers and all the executives at the Polus Group, and the professors at the Harvard Business School. As people move issues from the unsaid to the said, they occur to themselves to be more able, more powerful, more connected to each other. They move from being resigned (part of a racket) to inspired. Their business cultures, operations, and profits jump. Projects that once seemed impossible are now within reach. This is the essence of transformation: shifting the context and substance of people's lives and businesses, transforming everything, including oneself.

When we visited the Polus Group again in 2007, Keitaro had found himself as a strategist and CEO. He said that "while there are new problems and challenges, the issues of the past have disappeared."

Akio told us, "The biggest thing that came out of the program is that we were able to talk. I am listened to. The board and managers not only require my opinion, they actually want it." He spoke with confidence, offering ideas and making declarations about the company strategy.

In 2007, Nakauchi's widow (the mother of the three boys), who had sold bananas in the streets of Tokyo all those years ago, said, "It was dark after my husband's fall, but things have really lightened up a lot. The boys became leaders, the company has grown, and the family is closer together. I am happy."

Currently with more than two thousand employees, the company is on a growth spurt, with revenues of 110 billion yen (close to $1 billion). Of equal importance to employees, the Polus Group continues to receive more than its share of awards for design, environmental responsibility, and community relationships.

Where Performance Lives

The Polus Group and the Harvard Business School examples reveal that people often look for performance gains in the wrong place: in trying to force conversations before making space for them. We've seen that the way to make space is to leverage the fact that how situations occur arises in language—and in fact, the key to performance lies in language. In particular, dampeners to performance live in the unsaid, especially in the unsaid and communicated but without awareness.

There are specific actions leaders can take to tap into the power of the Second Law of Performance:

- Become aware of your persistent complaints, about people and situations. Notice that these cycle through your internal voice.

- Notice that these complaints are interpretations of facts, not facts themselves.

- See all four elements of rackets: the persistent complaint, the set way of behaving, the payoff, and the cost. See your rackets at work. We all have them.

- Probe into the situation by writing down everything you need to say to others, including anything you need to say, anything you need to forgive or be forgiven for, anything you need to take responsibility for, or anything you need to give up (including the complaint itself).

- Communicate what you discover to others in your work and life. Many people find that this action has a dramatic impact on performance.

In the next chapter, we'll explore what to do once you have created space: how to invent a new future that transforms how situations occur for people, leading to breakthrough performance.

3

Rewriting a Future That's Already Written

In May 1997, Malcolm Burns, a wiry, intense but soft-spoken Australian, walked to the front of a room filled with a hundred executives, managers, and union leaders, and said something so loud and surprising that many wondered what had happened to the managing director of their company, BHP New Zealand Steel.

Most of the people in the room knew Burns only through his reputation. When he first arrived at the company, the local newspaper had tagged him "Slash and Burns" because of his reputation for cutting costs and workforce size. Many of the managers and employees had believed he would close the plant.

The plant had seemed preordained to fail, and closing it seemed to be the obvious thing to do. The plant, too small to benefit from large economies of scale, produces relatively expensive steel. Unlike most companies that make money by selling steel "in country," BHP New Zealand exports two-thirds of its product, subjecting it to international market fluctuations. Between 1989 and 2004, the international price of steel declined to record-low levels.

As Ian Sampson, the head of human resources for the plant, told us:

When you think about it, we were expecting the impossible from the employees. Headcount was going down, change was everywhere, and the business was built on shaky technical assumptions. It was widely known that we might close down entirely. And yet we needed people to become proactive, positive, energetic, and to dramatically change their relationships with each other.

In the meeting, Burns started:

I think we've done a lot of good planning and efficiency work, but it won't get us to success. I've been sitting here, thinking about what will. It gives me a problem. I now know we need a future that excites us, and I'm not the kind of guy that can do that. I'm an operator. I love making things work, but I'm not a visionary. I can't come up with that future.

I'm going to put together a process that'll allow everyone to collaborate on creating the future that we need. I do know this—I'll know it when I hear it.

His tone was fiery and passionate as he declared:

Once we have it, if you work with me to make it real, you'll be my partner. If you don't, I'll fight you like an alley cat. In fact, I'll fight like an alley cat with anyone at headquarters who doubts our future, with any politicians whose actions and policies are damaging to our future, with customers and suppliers who are not supporting us for the future, and anyone else in the community whose words or deeds are likely to create problems for our future.

As the audience's reaction went from shocked to excited, many rising to their feet and applauding, he stood and shouted, "And if you don't think I am living up to these commitments, *tell me!*"

Their quiet, technical manager had become an outspoken, articulate, and even charismatic leader. For the next year, he did "fight like an alley cat" with those who opposed the future that was created, and he partnered with those who supported the future. Burns had rewritten his own future; now he sought to rewrite the future of the company.

Two years later, the work was done. At 6:00 AM on a Saturday morning, six hundred employees gathered to say good-bye to the man who had not only kept the plant open but also allowed it to flourish. Safety performance had improved by 50 percent, key benchmark costs had fallen by 15 to 20 percent, return on capital had increased by 50 percent, and raw steel produced per employee had risen by 20 percent. All this had happened while the workforce was reduced by 25 percent in a positive, constructive, and cooperative manner. The company kept up the momentum, and today is branded as the world's only boutique steel producer.

During the farewell ceremony, after a prayer from the plant chaplain and blessings from the local Maori tribes, Burns presented the whole workforce with a steel wall sculpture made from product in the plant, in the shape of an alley cat. It is now hung with pride in a place in the conference room where all can see it and be reminded of its significance as they continue the company's transformation.

What produced this turnaround? Was it some charismatic quality that Burns developed? Was it the relationships that he forged? Was it process improvements that were implemented?

Throughout history, a few exceptional people have produced results that left others scratching their heads about what had happened. In most cases, their followers aren't able to do what they had done, which makes their efforts occur as all the more unusual.

We spent years studying people like Burns and situations like New Zealand Steel, where the results continued after the leader moves on. The purpose of this chapter is to make what he did available to a wide group of people.

What we learned is that dramatic gains in performance *always* stem from a shift in how the situations occur to people, as captured by the Third Law.

The Third Law of Performance

Future-based language transforms how situations occur to people.

The Third Law rests on a fundamental distinction: there are two different ways to use language. The first is descriptive—using language to depict or represent things as they are or have been. The test of good descriptive language is whether it accurately articulates the world as it is, whether people see the world rightly. Descriptive language is often used to look back, spot trends, and predict what will happen.

Descriptive language is useful and important—try getting around New York City without a map, or ordering dinner without a menu. How would you feel if your surgeon couldn't describe the procedure about to be performed on you, or if your stockbroker couldn't describe your portfolio?

Descriptive language has its limits—you can't create something new by merely describing what was and is. Using descriptive language to talk about the future is limited to prediction based on past cycles and current realities.

The Barbados Group was intrigued when a result surpassed what seemed possible. In all of the situations that we studied, the way people talked and communicated was not descriptive. There was little or no prediction. People crafted new futures that were not likely to happen, but that they committed to anyway. People were talking in a way that we call *future-based*.

Future-based language, also called *generative language*, has the power to create new futures, to craft vision, and to eliminate the blinders that are preventing people from seeing possibilities. It doesn't describe how a situation occurs; it *transforms* how it occurs. It does this by rewriting the future.

The Power of the Future

We can now go more deeply into the future—where it comes from, what sustains it, and how generative language can rewrite it.

You can see the power of the future in the question, *Does money make you happy?* Most people say no, but the answer is more complicated. Take two families. One made $200,000 last year; the second, $50,000. Next year, both expect to earn $100,000. The first will be unhappy, and the second, happy. Why? Because it's not the actual money you have today that makes you happy or unhappy; it's the money you expect you'll have, believe you'll have, hope you'll have, or fear you'll have that shapes your experience of money right now. The first family will cut back, maybe sell their home. The second will buy a bigger house, take a vacation, and get a new car.

A universal principle becomes clear in this example: people live into the future they see coming at them, not the actual future they'll get to someday. Unless people have done something radical to alter their course, the future they are living into is their default future. By *default future* we don't mean the inevitable future—such as aging and eventually dying—but rather what is going to happen *in our experience*, whether we give it much thought or not.

Our default future consists of our expectations, fears, hopes, and predictions, all of which are ultimately based on our experience in the past. Incidents from the past live on as prediction, giving us our default future.

When we interviewed employees at New Zealand Steel about their default futures, as individuals and as groups, the picture was consistent: the plant would close, the economic effects would devastate the tiny community, some people would go on welfare and never work again, other people would move and never return. The people at New Zealand Steel lived into the default future by fighting Malcolm Burns, threatening walkouts, and strengthening the unions.

At the Polus Group in Japan, the default future was that the company would never again be the vibrant, driving force it had been. The sons would do their best, but without their father to lead them, the company would lose its momentum, slowly declining in prominence and profitability. Some smaller form of the company would survive, but its best days were behind it. The people of the Polus Group lived into this default future by squabbling and putting in less than their best effort.

At Lonmin, the case in Chapter One, the default future was one of conflict, with the unions fighting each other and management. Deaths from AIDS, homicide, and mine accidents were unpreventable and inflicted an unrelenting grief on the community. The people of Lonmin dealt with this default (and almost certain) future by fighting for a bigger share of the resources and going on strike.

Again and again, the default future is a projection of what happened in the past, all told through descriptive language. Without generative language, people attempt to fight the future, paradoxically making it even more likely. Remember: whatever we resist, persists.

Notice that the default future has a lot to do with how situations occur in the present. Unless we do something—something other than fighting the future we see coming—it becomes the *default* setting. It will happen, no matter how much we don't like it or try to resist it.

The Power of Future-Based Language

Future-based language projects a new future that replaces what people see coming. It doesn't modify the default future; it replaces it. The future goes from the default to what our editor Warren Bennis calls an *invented* future.

Future-based language is responsible for historical moments becoming turning points. Benjamin Franklin is credited with having invented the word *American* and, in so doing, transforming thirteen warring colonies into a nation. His words displaced what most political analysts of the day predicted was inevitable—that the colonies would never speak with one voice. When Martin Luther King Jr. said, "I have a dream," he created that dream in others—and displaced the default future of racial segregation.

After the works of Franklin and King, people who listened to what they said saw a new future, one that had not been included in the default future. Ultimately, as the words of Franklin and later of King took root in the American consciousness, people found themselves drawn into a new future and acting to bring it about. The future they lived into had transformed, as did their actions.

When fifty-two men wrote and signed the Declaration of Independence, the future of a nation was created. The writers of that document didn't describe a new future. They declared the future of a new nation, one that was a break with the past and the beginning of a unique social experiment. (To make this point through an absurdity: imagine the impact the Founding Fathers would have produced if they had titled their document the Description of Independence.) Today, Americans are the future these fifty-two men created over two hundred years ago.

In World War II, the way the conflict occurred to the British was transformed by Churchill's speeches. Across the Atlantic, Americans' perceptions of the war were reshaped by Roosevelt's famous fireside chats. It wasn't because Churchill and Roosevelt fed people a positive spin on what was happening. In fact, people saw the difficult truth of the situation, but at the same time the leaders invented a future in which victory was unfolding in the midst of hardships. Churchill and Roosevelt were not trying to temporarily energize the citizens and soldiers of their countries. They were generating, in their speaking, a future worth living into, even when the situations and circumstances seemed gloomy and treacherous. Future-based language is generative in its ability to invent what didn't previously exist.

Churchill and Roosevelt's passion and determination went far beyond motivational speaking. A motivational speech pumps up a crowd for an hour, then dissipates as life gets back to normal. Motivation makes people feel good about themselves, maybe even inspired. But those feelings don't replace the default future that they're living into.

The act of creating a new future displaces whatever default future was already there. It has staying power.

Let's turn to your performance challenge. Think back on how the situation occurs to you. Notice that, even without trying, you think of past events. Your inner voice describes them and, based on what happened, predicts whether they will happen again or not.

Consider the future in more detail, for yourself, your relationships, your family, and your company. What will happen if things continue on as they have been? Are you resisting or fighting to make something happen or not happen?

Does your default future have any space in it to create something new, or is it all filled up?

What if, right now, you could substitute that future with another? Not one based on what's happened before, but something new? What if the future you see coming were to alter in its substance, going from default to invented?

Also, notice the connection between your future and how situations occur to you. See that if you rewrote your future, you would live into it *now*. Rewriting your future alters how situations occur in the present.

Imagine being one of those people who could create a future that you and others would live into, for years or decades. Doing so requires that we fully create a blank space and then make declarations into that space.

The Condition Required for Future-Based Language

You can't paint a picture on top of a picture on a canvas. You can't write a sentence on a page that is filled up with writing. You can't create a future when there is already one coming at you. Before anything is to be created, there has to be a space of nothingness. The canvas must be empty; the page, blank; and the future that you were living into, somehow emptied out.

But how do you empty out the future that you are currently living into?

There are three dimensions to this process of "blanking the canvas," and people often move back and forth among them until they feel they have the room to invent something new.

The first dimension is *seeing that what binds and constrains us isn't the facts, it's language—and in particular, descriptive language.* We saw this part of the process in Chapter Two, as the family and executives at the Polus Group delved into the unsaid to get to issues about which they were unaware. As we saw, issues that lurk in the unsaid occur as facts. When we become aware of these issues and are able to address and articulate them, what had occurred to us as facts shifts to being interpretations. We're able to ask, Which interpretations give us the most power? Or the most freedom? Or the most self-expression?

The knots begin to release when we see that we are bound not by the facts of life but by knots of language. At the Polus Group, people couldn't change the facts of the founder's incapacitation, but they had something to say about their reaction to it. What seemed a certain future is now seen as only a possible future, and in that moment other possibilities start to arise.

The second dimension is *articulating the default future and asking, "Do we really want this as our future?"* In Chapter One, Brad Mills led the community (and himself) to see that unless something radical happened, the community would continue to be plagued by AIDS, homicide, mine accidents, and poverty—no matter how they tried to fight against it. At the Polus Group, people saw that the company would fade into obscurity. In both cases, people's default future shifted from cloudy to clear. As it did, people's reactions were unanimous: *we don't want that!*

At both Lonmin and the Polus Group, people had a vague sense that events were headed in the wrong direction. Once they stopped, took a breath, and probed to find out what default future they were living into, they could make a choice to construct a new future. Until people can articulate the default future—the future that's driving their lives—they can't make a choice to go in a different direction.

Earlier in this chapter, we suggested you take a moment and ask what your default future is, especially related to your performance challenge. Like executives at Lonmin and the Polus Group, you might now ask yourself, is this future what I really want? If it is, commit to that future and bring it about. If not, keep reading—the next section shows how to create something new. Until you can articulate the future and see that it isn't inevitable and necessary but is a construction of language, it's impossible to make a choice. Instead, we feel constrained and attempt to fight our way out.

Once people have moved through both parts of the process—seeing that the default future arises in language and that, unless something remarkable happens, it's where they're headed—they have the room to create something new.

Have you ever put your fingers into Chinese handcuffs, the kind that children play with? You put your fingers into the cuff and then try to pull out and all that happens is that they tighten. The harder you pull, the tighter the trap. Paradoxically, the way out of these handcuffs is to push deeper into the trap. Then the trap releases.

Likewise, the more that you can say the truth about the future you're living into, the more you are released from the negative constricted bindings in your life and business—and the more room you have to create something new.

The third dimension to creating a blank space is the most powerful: *completing issues from the past*. It is the subject of the next section.

Completion: Generative Language That Creates Space

In the 1990s, consultants ran leadership sessions in Peru's Tintaya Cooper Mine, fourteen thousand feet up in the Andes. Originally opened as a government mine in 1985, it was bought by Magma Copper Company during the privatization movement in 1994. Prior to the purchase, it had been able to negotiate only one-year labor agreements with each of its two labor unions. The result was a constant state of argument, divisiveness, and contention. At times workers weren't paid, and they resorted to desperate means. On one occasion the union kidnapped a senior executive as ransom for their wages, and in the process of "negotiating" made him walk on his knees to a church in the center of the town to beg for forgiveness. The government responded to this and other incidents by sending in troops, and in the unrest that followed, several people were killed and others hurt. One man who was merely a bystander was shot in the face and permanently disfigured.

As his wounds turned to scars, this man made a series of decisions to deal with the wrongness of what had happened. First, he decided that what happened to him was not only tragically unfair, but part of an unfair system. Second, he would never again allow such a thing to happen. Third, to make sure he would never be harmed again, he would hold a constant vigil against anyone in authority.

Although he made these decisions about what happened in the past, they were actually decisions about the future. He couldn't listen to the idea that the future could be different from the past. His default future was cluttered with the results of decisions he made, occurring to him as fixed, closed, and determined.

Notice that the result was a racket—his complaint was that people treated him unfairly, and the consistent pattern of behavior was keeping vigil. There was a clear, two-part payoff: avoiding the domination of a situation, and being right. There was also a cost: vitality, self-expression, freedom, and joy.

Dealing with a racket requires the work we discussed in Chapter Two. We must become aware of all four parts: the complaint, the pattern of behavior, the payoff, and the cost. In most cases, it also requires *completing* an incident that happened in the past but now lives in the default future.

To *complete* means moving an incident from the default future to the past. This process goes far beyond "getting closure" or "starting the healing process." If you complete an incident, it no longer lives in your future. You remember it, and it can inform you, but it does not drive your actions. It also doesn't color how situations occur to you. You are free of it, permanently.

Think about your performance challenge. Is there anyone involved in the situation with which you feel distance? Perhaps any sense that something is off? From our experience, when people look, they know. What you're seeing are *incompletions*—something that lives in your future, some baggage from the past. One dictionary definition of *incomplete* is "lacking a part or parts, not whole." Another definition is "not concluded." The issue that is not concluded may be about your present company, a past company, even about another person or group of people. An incompletion lives in the occurring, not in the facts. Generally it lives in the unsaid and communicated.

As you continue to look for incompletions, look to see if anything triggers a sense of something missing, of distance, or of something that is not concluded. Some places you can look are resentments, regrets, integrity issues (such as broken agreements), lack of acknowledgment for your or another's contribution, or participating in gossip (which diminishes the person who was the target of the gossip).

You may become aware of an incident that you're conscious of but have been withholding. You may also sense that something is just off, but you can't put your finger on what it is. Either way, you can use future-based language to complete the incident.

There is no recipe for completion, but there is a basic movement of the conversation:

1. *Start a conversation with the person with whom you need to complete the issue.* Create a frame in which completing the issue is of benefit to the relationship.

2. *Address what happened—what you decided, what you did or didn't do, that's between you and the other person.* Because you've harbored it, you have to take responsibility for the diminishment of the relationship. It may even be to such an extent that you ask to be forgiven. Notice the use of language that is much more potent than descriptive: "I acknowledge taking responsibility for it." The very act of saying this is an action: acknowledgment is created in the moment you utter these words.

3. *Take whatever action is necessary, such as apologizing or giving up the racket.* When we give something up, forgive, are forgiven, a new space opens up. Again, this part of the conversation requires generative language, such as "I'm giving up the grudge I've been harboring for years."

Creating a new future requires a constant commitment to being complete with everyone involved. Doing so creates and sustains a blank space into which the new future can be created.

One question that comes up is, "What if I can't contact the person with whom I am incomplete?" In some cases, the person may have died. In the case of the man from Tintaya, he didn't know the soldier who had shot him. He completed the incident with mine president Lee Browne, who had no involvement with what happened but, in the mind of the man, represented the authority that had hurt him. Remembering that incompletions live in the occurring, you can find someone to stand in for the person. You might write down what you would say to the person if he or she were still alive, then read it as though the other person were there. If you do this, you will be surprised by how real it seems to be. Even though the person is dead, they continue to live in your experience.

As you examine your performance challenge, look to see what incompletions you have. Also look to see how you can start a conversation with the people in your business and life to complete the issue. Additionally, ask yourself if there's anything that can be done to demonstrate your commitment to completion.

Once Browne and the other executives learned how the man's face had been disfigured, they arranged and paid for reconstructive surgery. He was transformed from a cynical, hard-nosed person to a fully committed union leader. Because of his efforts, and those of many others, the entire company was altered. In the words of John Hetrick, the former head of Human Resources for Tintaya, "By applying the Three Laws of Performance, we not only transformed the company into a high-performance organization, we became the model for the rest of South America that fundamentally altered the industry for years to come."

You might also bookmark this page and reread the first story from Chapter One, about Antoinette Grib and Selinah Makgale. You'll see that what actually happened was that Makgale completed her resentment toward white, powerful women. Grib wasn't involved in the original incident, but she could stand in for the people who were. No matter what the issue is, how long it's lasted, or even whether the person involved is alive or dead, you can find a way to complete it. As you do, you're freeing up space in the future. In South Africa, people completed (for themselves) racism, homicide, exploitation, even apartheid.

It's worth pausing for a moment and considering our world with people all committed to getting and staying complete with one another. How would the world be different?

A step in bringing this vision about is to use discussion groups, or the online community at www.threelaws.com, to complete any issues you have. You can download a helpful guide on how to do this in groups from our web site.

Once the man from the Andes had completed the incident, he saw the managers in a new light; that is, they occurred to him in a new way. He could see that they were not the ones that had hurt him. For the first time, he could create a new future—for himself, for his relationship to the company, and for his relationship to the people he worked with.

Once the issue has been moved into the past, you will feel a draw to create something new and alive. Another form of future-based language is *declaration*, which is the subject of the next section.

Declaration: The Kind of Language That Creates a Future

All generative language relies on *speech acts*—an action taken through language.[5] The most fundamental of speech acts is a declaration, which brings a possible future into existence. A declared future is not a dream or a hope, but a future to which you commit yourself.

When you invest your money, it's money that is committed and at risk. When you invest yourself in a new possible future for yourself, your life, your relationship, or your company, you put yourself at risk. Why would you do that? Because creating a new future makes you the author of your life in a way few people have ever imagined.

Investing in yourself, putting yourself at risk, is essential in rewriting the future. We do this by *committing*, which is another speech act. We put everything we have at stake for the new future. When the fifty-two men created the Declaration of Independence, the document became serious business when they wrote at the end: "we mutually pledge to each other, our Lives, our Fortunes, and our sacred Honor."

Then they signed their names, literally committing their lives. In that moment, a war with England began.

This brings us to how inventing a future actually works. Just as a default future isn't certain, a created future isn't a done deal, either. What we invent is a *possibility*, to which we commit our entire being. The Declaration of Independence created the possibility of freedom, and people lived into that new future and pulled it toward them by picking up muskets and fighting. After the war was won, the invented future shifted from possibility to reality with the creation of the Constitution of the United States.

We can see all of these pieces, including commitment, come together as the Polus Group continued after the death of its founder.

Life After Stage 0: Creating a New Future

After the initial program, the family and executives of the Polus Group had the space to create a new future that would replace the default future of *no leadership because the founder isn't coming back*. They put together a team of sixty people, including themselves and senior managers from the three major divisions of the company.

The work began a few months later, in January 2002, and took six months to complete. The goal of the process was to develop a future in which every person had an authentic voice in the process. Unlike the way that most vision statements are constructed, there were no formulaic templates or consultants hard-driving a process. This future emerged from the group working for two full days a month for six months, often a roller-coaster ride of chaotic creative conversation and often agonizingly long alignment conversation.

The process in the room involved people making proposals, which were written and projected through a computer-generated screen. The facilitator would then check if anyone was not aligned with the proposal. Hands would go up, and one of the people was then chosen at random. Whoever was called on then had to come forward with a counterproposal. The two would interact until they aligned. The two would then ask if anyone else wasn't aligned. This process would continue until no hands went up.

This interactive and lengthy process continued until the group had produced not only a new future, but also a new business model that would deliver that future, and strategic outcomes in the year 2012 that would be the realization of that future. The outcomes included tangible measures of the future state to be realized.

Here is the future they designed in January 2002 (translated from the Japanese):

Powerful Future for Polus Group in 2012

Possibilities for Polus Group in 2012 are

1. Being a corporation creating a value of living that attracts attention from the whole world
2. Being a corporation so vibrant with life that new business projects are arising one after another through employees' idea and creation
3. Being the No. 1 popular and interesting corporation, a place where world-class businesspeople, students, and the children of our employees would love to work

We, the Polus future design team, promise to fulfill this future in whatever the circumstances will be.

After months of work, everyone aligned on this future. At that moment each and every person experienced enthusiasm rarely seen in an organization. People felt proud of what they had created, and the way the situation occurred to them shifted from *What are we going to do without the founder?* to *This is a powerful tribute to what the founder would have wanted.*

The future went from murky, with a twinge of impending dread, to a clear, committed vision, authored by the people themselves. Faces in the room altered, body postures straightened, and confidence and excitement lit up the room. The power that people were experiencing was illustrated by a comment of one of the senior managers: "I feel like a shogun must have felt."

What he said demonstrated a shift in relation to the future. In the Japanese culture (like others), only the boss—and the ultimate boss, the shogun—gets to call the shots. When we realize that we have the power to declare and commit to new futures, the world occurs as a world in which you are the shogun.

Until people at the Polus Group could write a future that they lived into and actively pulled toward them, they were stuck trying to patch an unworkable situation. By replacing the default future with their own creation, people collectively lived into an optimistic, exciting future. The old problems simply dropped away, and everyone's performance altered. The entire company transformed to become a vibrant firm, attracting the best and brightest, partnering with its community, and growing beyond anything the founder had imagined.

Most people don't see the potential of generative language because of the all-pervasiveness of descriptive language. Those who do often skip the foundation required to make it work. We now turn to the principles of that foundation.

Principles for Generating New Futures

Generating new futures is a radical departure from how executives usually lead change. Normally, top decision makers decide on a new strategy, often in concert with their consultants. The executives then travel around and attempt to achieve under-standing and buy-in. Even with their passion and persuasion, this usual approach doesn't shift how the situations occur to people, so it doesn't gain acceptance. Instead, people *talk about* the strategy. Nothing fundamental has shifted. Further, the default future is the same, and it overwhelms the executives' best intentions and efforts.

Principle 1: Futures Inspire Action

Creating a new future with a large group of people takes a radically different path; more important, it starts with a differ-ent intention: to displace nonproductive conversations with conversations that establish a future so vibrant that people are eager to bring it about. That future creates a sense of urgency, and people's actions correlate to it. People find themselves doing things that formerly would have occurred as impossible. All of this comes together in extraordinary performance.

The following question is at the heart of designing appli-cations for generating new futures: what conversations in the organization are missing that, if created and implemented, would leave people with new pathways for action? For those interested in organizational leadership, we'll go further into this idea in the next chapter.

Every organization, like every person, is unique. The artistry is in knowing where to begin, so as to accelerate the spread of a future that pulls people toward it, one that contains new possibilities, new levels of results that can be achieved, even new levels of fulfillment and self-worth.

Principle 2: Futures Speak to Everyone in the Process

Doug Young, a Northrop Grumman vice president, is one of the new leaders of the effort to get vehicles into space. His face conveys deep intellectual curiosity. With his precise gestures, he demonstrates the kind of exactness that's required to manage the millions of details his work requires.

In 2001, Northrop Grumman's strategists recognized that, to keep growing, the company needed to expand into markets other than defense. Space exploration became the obvious opportunity. According to Young, "We could leverage what we did in the defense market. We were investing in this new market, and [at the time] NASA was looking for alternatives to the legacy providers."

After four days of work with seventy people, using the Three Laws of Performance, Young was surprised—the outcome went beyond his expectations. In his words, not only did people "move through a difficult time" and "create a real team," but more surprisingly, "we defined our role within the company and the new marketplace. We suddenly found ourselves being a credible prime contractor for the next Apollo program ... a very positive experience."

During the session, one of the participants came forward at a break and said, "I came [to this facilitated process] because I had to. However, during our discussion, I remembered why I got into this business, which was space travel." For him, that mission was bigger than any company or competitor. "Now I'm turned on again," he said. "We are going to travel in space!"

What made this effort successful—besides what we've already discussed—is that people felt that the new future satisfied their concerns. Aerospace engineers, like everyone else, enter into their profession seeking to make a difference. A new future that is compelling offers the opportunity to make a difference, individually and collectively. The aerospace engineer who said "I'm turned on again!" found that opportunity. When everyone finds themselves in this situation, people pull together for the realization of that future and for each other's success.

Over time, the motivation that inspired the people at Northrop Grumman would ebb and flow, but the future was there to stay.

Principle 3: Futures Exist in the Moment of Speaking

At another mine owned by Magma Copper, executives, managers, and union officials were engaged in rewriting their future. A heated argument broke out about whether or not "being a family" should be part of their declaration. One executive held out, saying that family has nothing to do with business. As he elaborated on his opposition, he said, "I can't fire people in my family!" After hours of back-and-forth discussion he realized that "it's more important that this group own the result" than anything else. He said to the group: "I don't know what I was thinking. We *are* a family!"

The room exploded. Everyone stood up cheering. It was as though a hundred people were suddenly speaking with one voice. By declaring themselves *family*, the *experience* of family occurred in the room, and that experience became a critical element of the company's future.

Future-based language doesn't describe anything in the current reality. Rather, it creates a possible future to which the speaker is giving their word *in the moment of speaking*. For example, when a justice of the peace says, "I pronounce you husband and wife," a marriage is created in the moment of speaking, and a new future is established for the couple. When people signed their names to the Declaration of Independence, the possible future we came to know as the United States of America was created.

Take a moment and speculate about a future for yourself and others that would

- Inspire action for everyone involved
- Fulfill the concerns of everyone involved—yourself, your family, those you work with
- Be vibrant and compelling in the moment you say it

As in New Zealand Steel, the Polus Group, and Northrop Grumman, crafting a future takes time. It needs ideas and creativity from you and many other people. It's ready when everyone involved says, "This speaks for me!" and they give their word to make it happen.

Building Companies and Lives Around Futures

Malcolm Burns of New Zealand Steel was a remarkable leader because he allowed others to build a future that would inspire them. As that future developed, Burns became the walking embodiment of it. In contrast to leaders who create dependency, when Burns left New Zealand the company was self-reliant and self-generative. The people in the company and community were authors of their own future.

There are specific actions that leaders can take to construct a future that causes themselves and others to live into it:

1. Commit to the discipline of completing any issues that surface as incomplete.
2. Articulate the default future—what is the past telling you will happen?
3. Ask, *do we really want this default future?*

4. If not, begin to speculate with others on what
   future would (a) inspire action for everyone,
   (b) address the concerns of everyone involved,
   and (c) be real in the moment of speaking.

5. As you find people who are not aligned with the
   future, ask, *what is your counterproposal?*

6. Keep working until people align—when they say
   "This speaks for me!" and they commit to it.

Part Two takes the Three Laws into leadership: leading
others and turning entire organizations into global leaders. For
those readers not interested in organizational issues, we suggest
skipping to Part Three.

PART II

Rewriting the Future
of Leadership

With So Many Books on Leadership, Why Are There So Few Leaders?

A leader is most effective when people barely know he exists. When his work is done, his aim fulfilled, his troops will feel they did it themselves.
—*Lao Tzu*

This chapter is about the kind of leadership that arises from the Three Laws of Performance—leadership that has the power to rewrite the future of a group, an organization, perhaps a country. The result of such efforts is remarkable success, with the effect Lao Tzu foretold—leaders who act as catalysts, with people around the leader feeling they did the work themselves.

Becoming such a leader is no small task, in part because the experts don't agree on what leadership means, how to do it, or what it looks like when people get it right. Warren Bennis wrote in *American Psychologist* in January 2007, "It is almost a cliché of the leadership literature that a single definition of leadership is lacking." Joseph Rost went further when he wrote, in *Leadership for the Twenty-First Century*: "The scholars do not know what it is that they are studying, and the practitioners do not know what they are doing."

In spite of the confusion and contradiction among experts, some people do become leaders. In general, they have to confront the fact that almost everything they've come to know as leadership is, at best, something else—entrepreneurship, management, marketing, or personal discipline.

Paul Fireman is such a leader.

The Rapid Rise of Reebok

Paul Fireman was born in Boston, and, true to his Yankee roots, he's a tell-it-like-it-is straight shooter. With an accent like that of Matt Damon's character in *Good Will Hunting*, he comes across as a regular guy, although with energy and enthusiasm that set him apart. Fireman is genuine, funny, and without airs; he's always ready with jokes, stories, and parables. His warmth turns passionate when he talks about sales, marketing, and entrepreneurship.

As a teenager, Fireman developed a love for golf, working as a caddy. He now owns golf courses, and according to *Forbes* is one of the seven hundred richest people in the world. What makes his story so unique is that he built an empire through personal entrepreneurship, turned it over to "professionals," watched it decline, regained control, and rebuilt it through empowering others—and all, as Lao Tzu said, with people feeling that they did it themselves.

In 1979, Fireman, looking for a business opportunity, went to a trade show in Chicago and met a representative from a British athletic shoemaker called Reebok. The original Reebok company handmade four hundred pairs of track and field shoes a year. Intrigued by the product, Fireman became a distributor during the height of the running craze in the United States and, thanks to his sales savvy, he could tell the company had huge potential, so he bought it out in 1984.

After Fireman bought Reebok, the company teetered on the edge of bankruptcy. Fireman obtained $75,000 from a friend and put this capital into research and development. Fireman and his team discovered that people hated (though they also accepted) that buying new running shoes meant breaking them in—suffering the blisters that came with the process. Studying the love-hate relationship runners had with their shoes, Fireman discerned an unmet and unarticulated market need. The company's response was an alternative that they called the *aerobic shoe*—made with soft leather, lighter, and already broken in.

As Fireman tells the story: "We went to market, and retailers were intrigued, but not quite sure it was right, so no one would be the first to buy them. We ended up taking $50,000 worth of shoes to gyms in California and began to think of deals, like two weeks free at a gym with purchase of the shoes. We also gave free shoes to gym instructors."

The gambit paid off big-time. The instructors liked the shoes, people asked about them, and within four weeks Reebok had sold out its inventory.

After an eighteen-month ad campaign, the young company had 43 percent of the market share. Every six months, their business doubled, eventually surpassing Nike's market share in 1987 and becoming the dominant force in the market. Fireman described the company at that time as "perfectly aligned, working in one fluid motion, and at 98 percent productivity—it was beautiful."

Fireman's early success was due to entrepreneurial grit, personal passion, test marketing, and slow-to-respond competitors. He was the central focus in the company, trying to manage and direct everything himself. When the company went public, the board began to worry that Fireman was in over his head, especially as the company pushed into foreign markets. In 1987, Fireman did what some other entrepreneur-CEOs were doing in the 1980s. Like Apple's Steve Jobs; Ben Cohen and Jerry Greenfield, the ice-cream icons; and Mitch Kapor, the founder of Lotus, Fireman turned over control of the company to "professional management." Telling the *Wall Street Journal* that he "needed extra support," he named Harvard MBA Joseph LaBonte as Reebok's president and head of operations. Within two years the company's growth slowed, and Nike regained the number one spot.

During the next decade, Reebok had five presidents—all "professional managers"—and the result was cultural revolt and loss of market share. Without clear leadership or a common sense of a future, in Fireman's words, "we had no future." Execution suffered. Manufacturing encountered one glitch after another—such as when the company's Indonesian factory produced thirty thousand pairs of shoes for volunteers at the Atlanta Olympics, all a half size too small. Even product design faltered, as when the company launched a running shoe named *Incubus*, only to discover later that the name refers to a mythical demon who has sex with women in their sleep. For a company that built its success on women's shoes, these were major setbacks.

The new reality was about execution, and that had never been Reebok's, or Fireman's, forte. Years later, *Boston Magazine* quoted an analyst as saying: "Fireman [had] a hundred ideas at a time, with a hundred people under him telling him that they are all brilliant. And so you [had] this company where everyone is running around in a million different directions." Morale was down. In a game where sports ruled the day, Reebok was, in the words of the same *Boston Magazine* article, "coming up on halftime in what may be the final contest. And to hear some people tell it, [Fireman] is down by 20 points and has lost his shooting touch."

In the late 1990s, Fireman saw only one solution to preserve Reebok's future, and he had to take action. Fireman took back total control of the day-to-day operations of the company.

At the time, *Business Week* asked, "Can Paul Fireman put the bounce back in Reebok?" Fireman knew the person at the top needed to epitomize the values and passion of the company. The problem confronting Reebok was, in his words, that "we ran out of oxygen with new products, had no new development, and we were bogged down with self-imposed issues. We were fighting ourselves."

Throughout his career, Fireman's style had been to take bold action, guided by his values, instinct, and salesmanship. Unlike many successful entrepreneurs, Fireman was honest enough to know he was at the limit of what he knew. He sought to provide a new kind of leadership at Reebok, to return the company to what he called its "previous purity." Fireman wanted to create the future for Reebok. As he sought something new, he contacted Steve in 1994 and was captivated with the idea that leaders empower others to rewrite the future. Fireman said, "I knew the company was going in the wrong direction. We needed help in working together, and then we could move to changing products and R&D. We needed to change our process."

In 1995, he initiated the process of rewriting the company's future. He put together a group of diverse people from throughout the company—people whom other people listened to, regardless of their level in the hierarchy. He started the first meeting of what came to be called the Long-Range Planning Group by saying, "I'm offering you the opportunity to share with me the accountability of the entire enterprise. I'm inviting you to be accountable for the way Reebok is today, and how it can be tomorrow. I'm offering you the chance to take on this accountability, and share it with me, and that includes designing the future of Reebok and enrolling others and working toward alignment."

The design of the process ultimately involved five hundred people and created a five-year future for the company. One person involved in the process remarked, "In other companies, I'd get statements of future goals, and they were just words on a paper, like things I was supposed to do. But now I own the future, as though I wrote every word of it."

This feeling was widespread. Fireman was beginning to exercise leadership that empowered others to rewrite the future. During this intense, sometimes argumentative, often inspirational process, senior management began to work together. Fireman said they "were finally on board, were more positive, and were finally leading. We were able to change the 'professional management' culture back to alignment. We reinvigorated ourselves."

Fireman's leadership brought cutting-edge product design and development into daily discussions. Fireman said, "When I took over corporate leadership we had no future. I took the process and used it to get alignment. I worked with the two most important groups—marketing and R&D."

As Fireman told us:

There was no loss of momentum, morale, or focus. Working with the groups, plans changed on the fly. We displayed the agility we had before, in the late '80s. A lot of this happened under the radar of the press, especially after I had taken back 100 percent of the day-to-day control. We started to develop new products and new opportunities—DMX, the music shoes, and 3D technology. Our whole focus was to make products for the customer that would benefit them—not just create shoes because we could. We developed fresh ideas again, built our credibility again, and started to compete in the market again.

In 2005, seeing further consolidation in the industry and a way to compete head-to-head with Nike, Fireman led the sale of Reebok to Adidas for $3.78 billion.

The Three Leadership Corollaries

The question facing people who want to provide leadership is this: how can they join the ranks of Paul Fireman, and others we've met in this book: Malcolm Burns from New Zealand Steel, Brad Mills from Lonmin, and Doug Young from Northrop Grumman?

Each of the Three Laws of Performance has a message for leaders. Each has a leadership corollary—a corollary that guides what leaders do and, more important, shapes who they are for others. Just as scientists and engineers use the laws of physics to send a rocket to the moon, leaders can use the Three Laws to elevate performance even in situations that seem impossible.

As introduced in previous chapters, the First Law of Performance is *how people perform correlates to how situations occur to them*. From this, we get the following leadership corollary:

> ### Leadership Corollary 1
>
> Leaders have a say, and give others a say, in how situations occur.

Fireman's inclusion of many diverse stakeholders in creating the future of Reebok had a remarkable effect. Their view of each other, the company, and the possibilities for the future completely shifted, from a view based on resignation and cynicism to one of excitement, passion, and commitment. "Compliance" was replaced with authentic expressions of ownership and authorship for the future of the company.

Fireman told us: "A great leader inspires people to align, allows for alignment to occur. We struggled until we were aligned, over and over, until we knew who we were and what we were doing." During one of these alignment sessions, Fireman asked the group, "Standing in the future, looking back, what's missing?" The group concluded that seven projects would be needed. Five hundred people joined these seven groups, each establishing its own name, mission, measures of success, and process, as follows:

- "Nail the Number" (align individual targets with company objectives)
- "75 or Else" (save $75 million in expenses)
- "Project Hat Trick" (align marketing with the money spent on sports endorsements)

- "To SKU or Not to SKU" (determine the ideal number of SKUs, or product types)
- "In the Bag" (cut the time required to get concept shoes to salespeople)
- "A Stitch on Time" (improve the process for getting the salespeople apparel on time)
- "Honey, I Shrunk the Inventory" (cut inventory to 1994 levels)
- "Olympic Gold" (leverage the Olympics to make Reebok the most respected brand in the industry)

Participating in these projects was voluntary; that is, they were taken on in addition to each person's current job. Imagine how their sense of what was possible in working at Reebok must have shifted. The project names alone capture some of Reebok's spirit—competitive and fun—and show the spirit of partnership at work on the problems of execution.

Fireman notes, "Each step of the way was discovery— discovery of unmet markets, unexpressed customer needs, unresolved problems, how to build an ethical company in an industry known for unethical labor practices, and discovery of leadership—the type that would be required to serve the customers and empower the employees." People we interviewed in the company said they felt like pioneers. Even more remarkable was how people perceived their leaders, the future design process, and themselves.

Looking back, Fireman summarizes his two times at the helm of Reebok: "I feel that there were a lot of people who achieved things that they wouldn't have imagined possible in their life."

It's worth pausing and asking yourself whether you can say the same about your company, career, and life.

Most readers of this book are looking for radical elevations in performance in their organizations, going beyond fixing what's wrong or making things incrementally better. Leaders who empower others to rewrite and realize futures can transform any situation, no matter how "impossible" it may seem.

As a leader, you can't control or determine how situations occur for others, but you do have a say. Take a moment and ask these questions:

- How can I interact with others so that situations occur more empowering to them?
- What processes, dialogues, or meetings can I arrange so that people can feel like coauthors of a new future, not merely recipients of others' decisions?

Fireman not only had something to say about how situations occurred to people, but he also tapped the power of language to make an impact. The Second Law of performance is *how a situation occurs arises in language*. From this, we get the second corollary:

Leadership Corollary 2

Leaders master the conversational environment.

There's a story that illustrates this corollary:

In ancient Greece, Archimedes was in a tough spot. He had used his new invention—a lever arm and a fulcrum—to move boulders, cargo onto a boat, even a small house off its foundation. After looking at all he had done, he declared, "Give me a lever long enough and I can move the world."

The king heard the tale of his achievements and his boasting and decided to make an example of Archimedes. On royal orders, the largest ship of the day was filled with so much cargo that it barely floated. The king said it was immovable, and he ordered Archimedes to move it out of the water using his new invention—if he could—or face the penalty for idle boasting.

Archimedes approached the ship and studied it for half a day. He took a few notes, then left the dock. Archimedes came back early the next morning with lots of equipment. He set up a system of fulcrums and lever arms, with each smaller lever moving a larger one, the largest of all attached to the ship. At sunset, Archimedes pulled on one end of a rope attached to his maze of arms and levers. The "immovable" ship rose out of the water, to the amazement of the crowd.

Archimedes proved that some things that occur as immovable aren't. The key to performance, as we saw in Chapter Two, lies in language. The levers and pulleys that make even impossible situations malleable live in the conversations that exist or can exist in an organization.

Consider that an organization can be viewed as a network of conversations. While we're not arguing that this assertion is a true statement, we are suggesting it is a useful perspective for leaders to take. Again, our starting point is that an organization is its network of conversations.

It's useful to think this through. Is there anything that matters that isn't done through conversations? Conversations produce innovations. Conversations are the vehicle for delivery of services. Conversations coordinate activities.

Strategic plans, maps, memos, e-mails, pictures—these are all aspects or elements of conversation. Management meetings, department meetings, board of directors meetings are nothing more than extended conversations.

In most organizations, the network of conversations is noisy, conflicted, filled up with gossip and chatter that makes new futures impossible because they project a probable and default future that people are living into.

From the perspective of the Three Laws, leadership is empowering others to rewrite the already-existing default future and to realize goals that weren't going to happen. From this definition, 100 percent of leadership happens through conversations that pull people into the game, not through sitting back and creating visions that then need to be sold. Leaders who master using future-based language have power that others don't have.

There are two elements that the conversational environment needs to include to achieve breakthrough performance. The first is an ongoing and company-wide commitment to resolving any and all incompletions, as we saw in the last chapter. The result is an organization-wide "blank space" into which a new future can be created.

When thousands of people in a company clear out their individual and collective default futures, it's not the same company anymore. Imagine if, in your organization, everyone had cleared out their issues, so that there were no old grievances at work. Imagine your personal life—your family and friends—in the same condition.

As Paul Fireman told us: "When you work with people in leadership, as manager at the top, or as an employee, there are conversations that you don't agree with. If you don't get them cleared up, they just keep surfacing until you either get chaos where good people leave, or become bureaucratic."

In our experience, Fireman is on the mark. When people's futures are filled up with decisions from the past, managers tend to produce policies, procedures, rules, and systems designed to prevent the negatives that happened before—lawsuits, strikes, employees who steal, managers who abuse the privilege of their positions—from ever happening again. Organizations become multiperson versions of the man from Tintaya, described in the last chapter.

Leaders manage, and master, the conversational environment by working with people to resolve any incompletions they have. This process moves past issues from the future to the past, creating a blank space into which the new future can be created.

Leaders also work with other people to bring group rackets into the open so they can be discussed and resolved.

When Fireman regained day-to-day control of Reebok in the 1990s, his job was to get everyone's default future cleared out, so that a new future became possible.

In addition to creating a blank space, mastering the conversation environment means implanting the second key element: *integrity*. As our Barbados Group colleagues Werner Erhard and Mike Jensen are fond of saying, "Without integrity, nothing works."[6] Integrity creates a condition of workability; without integrity, effectiveness is diminished and displaced by broken promises and lack of accountability.

What is integrity? Webster's *New World Dictionary* defines it as "the quality or state of being complete; unbroken condition; wholeness; entirety," which we'll summarize as "whole and complete." Think of integrity not as a moral or ethical issue, but as a factor in workability. You don't want to drive over a bridge that lacks integrity—that isn't whole and complete. Doing so doesn't work, and it puts you in peril.

Leadership can't empower others to rewrite and realize new futures when the conversational environment isn't whole and complete. When people make commitments and then don't follow through, the situation is left incomplete and divided. To use one example from Reebok, what if the leaders on the "75 or Else" project committed to the goal—saving $75 million—and then ignored the project and went about their workdays as if nothing had happened? Investors would become frustrated. Employees, cynical. Such a situation doesn't promote workability.

Leaders spark and foster conversations for integrity, conversations in which:

- People are truthful and honest.
- People do complete work, very well—doing it as it was meant to be done, without cutting corners.
- People do what they know to do, on time, and what others expect them to do, even if they haven't said that they would do it.

The last bullet point often stops people. They ask, "How can integrity demand that I do even what I haven't committed to?"

There are many things you have probably never formally agreed to—not stealing money, or not creating off-balance sheet partnerships à la Enron. These may sound absurd, but consider that coauthor Dave Logan interviewed people who had been at Enron, and several said, "We never agreed to not do those things!" From the outside, such justifications seem insane, but the view from the inside is different. According to the First Law of Performance, how those situations occurred to the people involved correlated perfectly with the actions they took. Integrity didn't appear as a relevant issue to them.

Leaders constantly generate integrity by fostering conversations that make it alive and important for people.

Integrity, as we define it, is not simply keeping one's word—it is honoring one's word. What's the difference? When a person knows he won't be able to keep his word, he honors his word by making that situation known to all the people who will be affected. He deals with the consequences of not keeping his word, cleans up whatever messes have been created, and makes new promises that restore workability to the situation at hand.

What do leaders do when people don't do what they say they are going to do? Author Peter Block told us: "The rest of the team has to confront you with their disappointment. They have to let you know that you have let them down. . . . Maybe some covenant has been violated and so you must leave." Leaders do whatever is required to establish and maintain integrity as part of the conversational environment, starting with leading the person to restore his integrity.

We earlier defined integrity as "whole and complete." How does this definition relate to honoring one's word? Because how situations occur to people arises from language, it follows that a person occurs for herself and for others inside of the word she gives. When her relationship to her word is inauthentic, divided, and incomplete, then her relationship with herself is inauthentic, divided, and incomplete. If she wants to restore her sense of herself to one of being whole and complete, her pathway is through honoring her word.

As we mentioned earlier, having integrity is not a matter of morality or ethics. It's also not about being perfect. It's about making things work. Throughout the course of our lives, everyone—the authors of this book included—has participated in situations that lacked integrity, and each time we found that things didn't work. We took on dealing with our past breaks in integrity, from little white lies to big white lies in our relationships, to the excesses of the counterculture of the 1960s and 1970s, to gaming the system and doing what was expedient instead of what worked. As we learned these distinctions of integrity and applied them to our personal lives, clarity replaced confusion, and the opportunity to contribute to others became real. Cleaning up situations that lacked integrity was often difficult but always made an inordinate difference in workability. And the same lessons can be found over and over again in organizational life.

Integrity, then, as defined from the Three Laws, means honoring one's word, and it becomes the approach that creates workability.

Paul Fireman's mission required workability, so it's no wonder that integrity was a big part of the conversations that he sparked. One senior vice president at the time said, "Are we willing to stand by the principles [to which] we have committed? It's all good to speak of them, but what are the consequences if we don't? What will we face? We all want this—working and relating to each other—and those who are not willing or able to live within those boundaries shouldn't be here. The company has to make this commitment."

Another senior vice president added: "Our objective is to take five hundred people ... [and] work as a high-performance team and get someplace that doesn't seem possible."

Take a moment and reflect on the conversational environment in your business and life. Specifically, you might ask:

- What decisions from the past are in my future?
- How do the people around me relate to their word?
  Do they honor their word? Do I honor my word?
- How can I start new conversations that make
  integrity vibrant for others and myself?

In Chapter Seven we'll return to one idea in this corollary we haven't addressed: mastery. Mastering the conversational environment requires thinking from an unfamiliar place. Although mastery is a challenging commitment, the payoff in terms of performance, and of satisfaction for everyone involved, makes it more than worthwhile.

With the environment tended to, we now turn to the essence of leadership and the corollary to the Third Law of Performance: *future-based language transforms how situations occur to people.*

Leadership Corollary 3

Leaders listen for the future of their organization.

(The Three Laws of Performance and the Three Leadership Corollaries are presented together in the Appendix.)

Ray Anderson is a leader who epitomizes this third corollary. Although he had not been exposed to the Three Laws, we see the effect he had when he rewrote the future of his company.

As founder and chairman of Interface, the world's largest maker of modular carpet, he was enjoying the success of the company he built. In 1994, one of his sales representatives handed him a book, Paul Hawken's *The Ecology of Commerce.* In Anderson's own words:

> [The book] lands on my desk, so I begin to thumb it. About page 19, I came to a chapter heading "The Death of Birth," and I began to read what it was about. I read the ten pages, and it was a very emotional thing for me. I said: "Good God, what set me up for that book?" I was pretty sure at age sixty, I

must have subconsciously been asking myself, what is my child going to grow up to be? (Interface is my third child after my two daughters.) I was also asking myself if I belonged in the company, having hired lots of new successful management, and the company was doing well.

The book ... gave me a whole new purpose in life in my sixty-first year. I asked a task force to take the company to sustainability, to be the first in the industrial world to be a zero environmental footprint. To take nothing permanently from the earth, nothing permanently left behind. This was a tall order for a petrochemical chemical, nonrenewable fossil fuels, not just in materials, but also in the energy that creates our products.

One needs only to see Anderson interviewed or read about him to get a sense of who he is. He used future-based language to launch the next phase of Interface, and in a real sense he became that future. Since stepping down from the CEO role, he has been on a tear, making speeches, encouraging other corporate leaders to establish a goal of zero harm to the environment.

Early in our work, we sat with our editor, Warren Bennis. In talking about the Third Law of Performance, he became quiet, as if thinking about what it meant. After a moment, he said a few words that stuck with us: "Cicero talks, and people marvel; Caesar talks, and people march." Throughout time, when leaders speak, people are moved to action. This third corollary gives us insight into how ordinary people have become remarkable leaders by becoming the essence of the future.

Leaders create conversations from the Third Law, composed of future-based language, to invent futures for the organization that didn't previously exist. However, leaders don't rewrite the future by themselves—they create the space and provide the "listening" for that future. When the future coalesces, leaders have a way of knowing it; it's like the future goes "clunk" for them, like tumblers in the combination lock to a safe. Articulating what they just experienced becomes a matter of self-expression. Because leaders are intentional about giving others a say in how the future occurs for them, often the work of rewriting the future is done through an empowered group of people. These people own the future because they are its coauthors. There is no implementation problem (a big problem for organizations). Because the group has coauthored the future, you could say this future is implemented in the very being of the coauthors themselves.

Because leaders listen for a future that inspires them, they can trust their intuition. It's that certainty—that leaders will know the future when they hear it—that gives leaders from the future a remarkably strong compass. Leaders of such organizations, like Fireman, *are* that future, appearing as inspiring and energetic. Their power comes not from their personalities but from the future that is their mandate, their guide, and their reason for being. Rather than trying to figure out which future will call forth committed action, they trust this experience of the pieces coming together, going "clunk" for them. This ability is what we mean when we say that "leaders listen *for* the future."

How exactly does this ability develop?

Leaders listen for the future in the same way a physician searches for an effective diagnosis. The doctor examines the patient, blood work, X-rays, and history of present illness and reviews all the information. Most important, the physician listens to the patient and listens for a diagnosis, which eventually goes "clunk." Likewise, the leader looks at the present situation from a number of different perspectives, taking into account such aspects as finances, products, market position, competition, culture, and aspirations of employees. If the leader has tended to the environment (especially clearing out the default future and maintaining integrity), the leader has the space to listen for a future. This is leadership that literally has everyone talking—putting forward ideas, testing them, making proposals and counterproposals. Eventually, something goes "clunk" for the leader. It's as though the future appears in that moment for her.

It's a future that goes far beyond today's best practices of casting a vision and getting buy-in. The experience is that, in the moment, people begin to live into the future. It isn't a "someday, maybe" vision, but a future that is real in the moment. It compels action, because it transforms how situations occur for people.

Throughout this book we've seen leaders who listened for the future of their organizations. Brad Mills was listening for a future at Lonmin—he didn't write it himself, but he created the space in which others could act as coauthors. Malcolm Burns did the same at New Zealand Steel. So did Paul Fireman at Reebok, and Ray Anderson at Interface.

A leader who taps into the Three Laws listens for a future that will transform everything in the present. A leader listens for a future that is not predictable, probable, linear, and was not going to happen anyway, and which compels inspired action.

Take a moment and ask yourself these questions:

- If I wanted to cocreate a future with others, who would I need to involve?
- How would I need to listen to them?
- Where would I have to be willing to give up controlling a direction so a new future could arise?
- As you consider these questions, you might refer to all Three Laws and all Three Corollaries, in the Appendix.

Conclusion: Leadership—Rewriting the Script

Every leader we've examined in this book so far has had one thing in common: a present situation that appeared difficult, hard, even impossible. Every one sought to fix a set of problems—union relationships, finances, even vision for the company.

Instead of fixing the problems in patchwork fashion, they transformed those situations by rewriting the future. Let's look at this idea from another angle.

Imagine a play called My Life, or perhaps My Company.[7] In this play, you are the star, and your character is well rehearsed.

Remember Shakespeare's famous metaphor in As You Like It: "All the world's a stage"? What if he wasn't speaking in metaphor? What if your life and company weren't like a play, but were a play? Life would be nothing more than scenes, characters, and conversations with other characters.

Is that really any different from life as we know it? Is there anything that matters other than scenes, characters, and conversations?

Aristotle said every play has three acts: a beginning, a middle, and an end.

The first act of the play called My Life or My Company is your past. The second act is the present. The third act is your future. Most of us are hoping for a future that contains more power, satisfaction, richness, vitality, and success than the present—a future we intend and hope to get to "someday."

Of course, we never actually get to the "someday future." That is why it is a "someday future." It's someday, but not now. We live in the present and are always only in the present.

This "someday future" is part of the third act of the play. It's not the whole of the third act, but it is a critical part.

It is presented in the lines in which your character expresses your deep hopes and wishes for the future, as if desiring it hard enough will bring it about. The joke of life is that we keep running after this illusion called the "someday future," which never comes. And then we die.

If you look deeply into the third act of your play, into the part that lies behind the hope, you will see that who you are and what is possible is already written. You will see that all of the decisions that you made about yourself and your life are already there in the third act. Where did these decisions come from? From the first act of your life. How you decided to deal with life in the first act of your play is still alive and well; it lives in the third act. And even though we never really get to the third act, what's written there creates our experience of the second act.

Is there anything we can do about this seeming trap? Are we doomed to live out a second act that perfectly matches a third act that we don't want while pursing a "someday future" that never comes?

We know we can't rewrite the first act. That's already been played out.

We can't rewrite the current act—that's being played out right now. We can, though, rewrite the third act.

To rewrite the third act, we have to take several steps. First, we have to clear out of the third act everything that's already there, moving it back to the first act where it belongs. This creates an empty space into which something new can be written. In this process, the illusionary "someday future" disappears, as it existed only as part of projected hopes and fears from the past. Second, we have to build integrity into this rewriting process. To rewrite a new third act, we have to see our relationship to what we write as a matter of honoring our word.

The third act you write has to be consistent with the first act. For example, if you lost your legs in the first act of your life, you can't declare yourself to be a ballet dancer in the third act. But within that constraint of consistency, there are many possible futures—many possible third acts. What if we could write that third act not just with ourselves, but with others? Leadership is creating the environment in which people can write their third act together—a third act in which the authors can see their personal concerns, and the concerns of the others, fulfilled.

As we involve others, we listen for a future, not bound by present situations. When it goes "clunk," a new third act takes shape. It compels others, and us, as we live into it. The very nature of the second act, the act that you're currently in, transforms, from difficult or impossible to vibrant. It shifts from going through the motions to being filled with possibilities. This new third act is not a "someday future" but a future that you have in the present moment.

People who have gone through this process say your new third act lights up your life. Will this new third act ever become reality? Who knows? The real future is completely uncertain. But until the end comes (usually as a rude surprise), you will have a new kind of second act, with a compelling and invented future.

The question facing you as a leader is this: will you empower others to rewrite that future with you and, in so doing, create a new type of organization?

This new type of organization is the subject of the next chapter.

5

The Self-Led Organization

> Every organization must be prepared to abandon
> everything it does to survive in the future.
> —*Peter Drucker*

In 1917, industrialist Charles M. Schwab wrote the following in his book *Succeeding with What You Have*:

I had a mill manager who was finely educated, thoroughly capable and master of every detail of the business. But he seemed unable to inspire his men to do their best.

"How is it that a man as able as you," I asked him one day, "cannot make this mill turn out what it should?"

"I don't know," he replied. "I have coaxed the men; I have pushed them, I have sworn at them. I have done everything in my power. Yet they will not produce."

It was near the end of the day; in a few minutes the night force would come on duty. I turned to a workman who was standing beside one of the red-mouthed furnaces and asked him for a piece of chalk.

"How many heats has your shift made today?" I queried.

"Six," he replied.

I chalked a big "6" on the floor, and then passed along without another word. When the night shift came in they saw the "6" and asked about it.

"The big boss was in here today," said the day men. "He asked us how many heats we had made, and we told him six. He chalked it down."

The next morning I passed through the same mill. I saw that the "6" had been rubbed out and a big "7" written instead. The night shift had announced itself. That night I went back. The "7" had been erased, and a "10" swaggered in its place. The day force recognized no superiors. Thus a fine competition was started, and it went on until this mill, formerly the poorest producer, was turning out more than any other mill in the plant.[8]

Today, businesses still wrestle with how to boost productivity, but they also struggle with problems unknown when Schwab was building his empire. Twenty-first-century leaders also struggle with implementing advanced technology, access to capital, pricing pressures, global competition, community self-sustainability, and relationships with a diverse and global workforce.

Although much has changed, Schwab's simple action points the way to rewriting the future of organizations.

It's worth spending a moment on the question: what did Schwab really do? Without the Three Laws of Performance, we would say he created a public measurement system and boosted competition between shifts. But was there something else? Perhaps even something brilliantly simple?

From the perspective of the Three Laws, Schwab used one word—"six"—to create a new network of conversations that put the steelworkers into a new game, with a new future. The new game was "beat six heats," and, as evidenced by results, workers found the new game inspiring. The way situations occurred to them shifted, as did their actions.

This example shows how artfully the Three Laws can be applied. Schwab didn't launch a new program, create new systems, or implement new incentives. With one action that took less than a minute, he transformed how steelmaking occurred to the mill workers and, thus, their performance.

The Way Businesses Can Have It All

This chapter isn't just about the usual business goals—making more money, building shareholder wealth, or making smart investments. Nor is it just about the usual concerns of social and environmental activists—healing the earth, caring for employees in developing countries, or avoiding corporate wrongdoing.

This chapter is about a new approach to managing and leading, in which organizations, grounded in the Three Laws, unlock new purpose and capability to accomplish it all. They can achieve both wealth and social responsibility, both profits and environmental responsibility, both expansion and partnership with people who have felt exploited by corporations.

We start by looking at the crisis conditions that organizations are in today, how they got into this mess, and what ordinary people can do to remake their organizations into what we call *Self-led organizations*.

The Rise of Corporations as Individuals

In our view, the organization is the single greatest invention in the past few centuries, resulting in the coordinated activities and resources of people. Organizations have sent people to the moon, harnessed the power of the atom and built the microprocessor, connected the world through air travel and the Internet, and created a standard of living that was unimaginable even one hundred years ago.

Yet with all the amazing accomplishments of organizations, many of our current problems are fueled by a narrow-minded view of the scope and purpose of a specific type of organization: the corporation.[9]

A book about rewriting the future would be incomplete if we didn't turn the power of the Three Laws to the problems organizations face. This most powerful of human creations requires more than "change management." Emerging global imperatives call for transformation—altering the underlying structure of a corporation's sense of itself. As we've done so often in this book, we'll start with the default future—this time, of organizations. As we've seen before, the default future is a recycled version of the past, so to look forward, we start by looking back.

Seeing the default future of organizations requires us to revisit how modern corporations developed in the United States and then spread worldwide. In the 1800s, they were rare. Corporations were usually chartered by a government for a specific purpose and a limited amount of time. A corporation would build a bridge, for example, and then disband. After the U.S. Civil War, Congress passed the Fourteenth Amendment, extending basic human rights to former slaves. In the decades that followed, business advocates convinced the U.S. courts to treat corporations as if they were individuals, with many of the same rights that individuals enjoyed. Corporations gained the right to employ people, own property, and sue and be sued, but unlike people, a corporation can't be thrown in prison, and it can continue to exist as long as it makes a profit.

In the past two hundred years, the capital markets have developed ways of buying and selling ownership in large companies in real time. This gave investors options—if they didn't like how a company was performing, they'd sell. After all, why would investors keep their money in a corporation, which could go bankrupt, unless they were getting a higher return than they would on safe investments, like government debt? To survive, corporations *had* to both earn a significant profit and grow that profit quickly.

To satisfy growth needs, corporations learned to leave the costs of their activities for others to pay. As they extracted resources from the earth, converting them to some other form, the environmental and human damage of their operations usually fell on governments and communities in the developing world. This process is called "externalization"—making costs external to the company. Because most corporations were playing the same game, a company that didn't externalize costs would be uncompetitive and might be abandoned by both customers wanting cheaper prices and investors seeking higher returns. The world became aware of the negative effects of externalization in the financial crisis of 2008, when bad debt created by corporations required government intervention to avoid economic collapse.

In 2004, Joel Bakan wrote and cocreated with Mark Achbar the documentary *The Corporation*, which chronicles corporate culpability in environmental damage, worker exploitation, and even criminal activity. With what Bakan told us was a bit of creative license, he and his filmmaker colleagues, Achbar and Jennifer Abbott, pose a question early in the film: "If a corporation is a person, what type of person is it?" They show that corporations often demonstrate:

- A callous unconcern for the feelings of others
- An incapacity to maintain enduring relationships
- A reckless disregard for the safety of others

- Deceitfulness: repeated lying and conning of others for profit
- An incapacity to experience guilt
- A failure to conform to social norms with respect to lawful behaviors

A person that exhibited these qualities would be clinically diagnosed as a psychopath.

As Ray Anderson said, people will look back centuries from now and say externalization allowed corporate leaders to become "plunderers of the planet."

Why the Heat Is Rising on Organizations

What worked in the past is no longer working, because the world is running out of places to hide. Not only are people (including shareholders) paying more attention to companies' role in climate change, but local populations are now armed with technology straight out of James Bond. People who didn't have newspapers now have cell phones that can access profitability data on their employers. Workers who are angry can capture video of their conditions and upload it to YouTube for the world to see—and to judge. Local communities are flexing more power, in some cases revoking companies' right to operate in their regions and countries.

Barring something unforeseen, these pressures will increase over the next decade, and as they do, businesses will find it harder to operate in certain parts of the world. Community self-sustainability and the strategic implementation of social responsibility will become the next major challenges for organizations. In fact, many developing and developed countries have enacted laws and regulations making improvements in these areas a requirement for the right to continue doing business. Externalization is becoming harder, while investors' demands for profits and growth are increasing. Add to this the fact that employees in all parts of the world are demanding better places to work—both in terms of working and living conditions. If a company doesn't promote sustainable practices, jobs in those companies occur as less valuable, and people's work as less important.

Uncertainty has crept into the very nature of what it means to be a company. Many leaders we talked to in organizations expressed a similar theme:

We're getting squeezed. We have to make our numbers and be good citizens at the same time. Sometimes you can't have it both ways, but it seems that unless we do, we will be out of business.

Leaders in other types of organizations are feeling the pressure from these trends as well. Governments need to raise revenue and protect the environment. NGOs often try to partner with companies as they criticize their actions. Start-ups compete with established ventures.

As management expert Peter Senge told us: "The world of the organization is changing profoundly, and no one is sure of the new rules."

We refer to this looming crisis as the *global warming of organizations*. The heat on organizations is getting turned up, and there's no relief in sight.

Rise of the Self-Led Organization

Leadership consultant Peter Block posed a question in an interview with us: "Can a collective organism like an organization have a purpose, other than growth, and can it bring something into the world that didn't exist before?" His answer to his own question was "Probably yes." He went on to say that a vision for organizations that would make a difference is clear, and it has been articulated by experts like Margaret Wheatley, Chris Argyris, and Peter Senge. "But we haven't been able to institutionalize that vision," Block said, "and so it remains elusive."

Although the last few decades have seen corporate responsibility increase, the fundamental nature of organizations hasn't transformed. As Gary Hamel wrote in *The Future of Management*, management of organizations has changed little since early in the twentieth century when the modern techniques of job descriptions, divisional structures, and decision rights evolved. Hamel noted that if management pioneers Alfred Sloan or Fredrick Taylor were alive today, they would see much that is familiar in how the current Fortune 500 operates.

The questions are: What would an evolution of corporations look like? What could the corporation of the late twenty-first century look like? How can we build them today, and use them to release us from crises we seem to be facing?

Before software developers release a new version of a product, they usually ask what users want that the current version doesn't provide. If they're savvy businesspeople, they'll also ask what new approaches will delight customers. So let's ask that question about corporations: What do users (investors, employees, customers, suppliers, governments, activists, non-profits, and union leaders) want that the older and outdated version doesn't offer? What new features would not just satisfy them, but delight them?

The twentieth-century organization was built on the analogy of corporations as individuals. The problem, we assert, is that the analogy wasn't taken far enough. Evolving this idea means extending the analogy in ways that, to our knowledge, have never been done before.

To be clear, we are not saying that corporations (or other types of organizations) are people. They're not. We are suggesting that the analogy of the corporation as a person has value we haven't mined yet—so much value that we can finally build organizations that have it all: higher profits alongside of authentic social responsibility. These organizations will have both an engaged, satisfied workforce and productive relationships with all stakeholders.

Being Self-Led

As we start to walk down the road that will lead us to the next version of organizations, think about what it means to be a person. What aspects of the human experience are most important to you? The right to own property, employ people, sue and be sued—the ways in which corporations are individuals today—would be on the list, but probably near the bottom. At the top of your list, we're willing to bet, would be values, aspirations, and elements that are noble—family, relationships, community, even joy and love. Our lives without these aspects would seem stark. Most of us seek a fully integrated experience, in which what we do every day is infused with, and guided by, these noble aspirations.

Notice that these aspirations are, at least in part, linguistic. Love, community, and relationships don't exist in the world independent of language.[10] Only human beings, with their linguistic nature, can live a principle-centered existence.

Our approach, from the Three Laws, is to consider the entire human experience as arising in language. We assert that this way of approaching what it means to be human gives a pathway to fully integrating our lives with our aspirations. It also gives us insights that are the basis of creating the next version of the organization.[11]

A person whose word is divided or split lacks wholeness and completeness. An enduring sense of satisfaction requires living with integrity—honoring our word, as we saw in the preceding chapter. Integrity—speaking consistently in all situations, keeping our word when possible, saying when we won't be able to keep it and then dealing with the consequences—makes us whole, complete, and powerful.

Most of us use language in a way that is fragmented. We seek to be liked, or win approval, or avoid situations that occur to us as dominating, and so we speak in a way that will bring us acceptance or recognition or safety *in that moment*. In another moment, with another group, we speak differently and create a lack of consistency and ultimately of power. We don't speak honestly, we hold back, we give our word and don't keep it. The result is a lack of integrity and a loss of power.

Most of us don't consider the effects of a lack of integrity in our lives. As we saw in Chapter Four, the list includes a loss of satisfaction, freedom, and self-expression. Consider also that a person lacking integrity lacks a single, integrated self. This idea is not new. The compilers of the *Stanford Encyclopedia of Philosophy* note the following: "Integrity is primarily a formal relation one has to oneself."[12] The same article mentions "Integrity as Self-Integration." In fact, this theme runs through the philosophical discourse on integrity—relating integrity to being whole and complete as a person.[13]

On the positive side, honoring our word is also the route to creating whole and complete social and working relationships, and it provides an actionable pathway to earning the trust of others. It allows who we really are to come forward and to become a presence in the world. We call such a person *Self-led*.[14] Self, with a capital "S," represents a full integration of all of the parts of a person, including those driven by principles, values, nobility—the highest aspirations. Integrity allows a person's Self to emerge and holds it in place.

It's key to remember that Self arises in language, through conversations.[15] Once we have an integrity-based relationship with our word, we can use conversations to build lives around this Self, resulting in greater effectiveness, purpose, capability, and satisfaction.

A person who is Self-led occurs as honorable, focused, confident without arrogance, wise, consistent, thoughtful, and dedicated. From different points of view, a Self-led person would be described as enlightened, integrated, or evolved.

The purpose of this chapter is to make an organization Self-led, with the Self arising from all those people participating in the organization's network of conversations. The result is an organization that has it all: skyrocketing profits, dedicated and engaged employees, satisfied local communities, and sustainability.

The New Organization: Built from the Self Up

Most organizations comprise networks of conversations that are inconsistent, dissonant, and cluttered. Think of the kinds of conversations you hear at work. The following will seem familiar:

Why are they doing that to us?

Will this be a good quarter? What's Wall Street going to think of us?

Are the rumors true?

My product is better than their product.

I just want to do a good enough job to not get fired.

I want to do a job that makes me proud.

I wish they'd appreciate what I just did for him.

How'd that person get so far ahead?

If a single person engaged in so many contradictory conversations, we might describe him as schizophrenic, paranoid, or psychotic. We certainly wouldn't count on his word or look for his leadership.

However, if an organization's network of conversations could be infused with integrity, and harmonized, we'd have the effect we saw with Lonmin, New Zealand Steel, the Polus Group, and many other cases in this book. All of those organizations found their Self and became Self-led.

For an organization to deal with the pressure cooker it is in, it needs to rewrite its future by altering its network of conversations. It needs to create a compelling future for its stakeholders and align its network of conversations to fulfill that future. In the process, the organization's Self emerges, which is the collective essence of all of the people involved in its operations, including a future that inspires them and fulfills their concerns. This is what we mean by a Self-led organization.

Although a process as complex as finding an organization's Self can't be reduced to steps, there is a critical flow, detailed in the following section.

Leaders Step Forward

The big question is, why don't more leaders step forward? Peter Senge gave us one reason: "We all have a sense of what is happening, a deep uneasiness. But we have become habituated to the modern artifacts of successful living, so we keep ourselves distracted and entertained—so we don't pay much attention."

Jim Collins, who suggests that what prevents many organizations from becoming "great" is a focus on being "good," alludes to another reason more leaders don't come forward. Only when they abandon holding on to being good can they move up to great. Likewise, people have to see beyond their current success before they can lead the effort of transforming an organization.

Finally, many people feel they don't have the authority to step up and make a difference. Yet in most of the companies in this book, the desire for "something more" began with people other than the CEO or chairman. At Interface (where Ray Anderson was the chief executive), it started with customers asking what was the company's policy on the environment. At Lonmin, it started with the communities demanding a different relationship with the platinum mine. At New Zealand Steel, it began with a concerned manager in Human Resources. At the Polus Group, it started with one employee taking a public Landmark Education program and wishing to apply what he learned at work. At Northrop Grumman, it started with a vice president.

A middle manager can, in our experience, use future-based language to create a case for taking new kinds of action that senior executives find compelling. It doesn't take authority to set an organization on a new course. It does take owning the situation, and knowledge of how to use the Three Laws to transform even psychopathic or self-centered organizations into star global citizens.

The first part of stepping up begins with standing for the possibility that your organization can go beyond its current views of success to a place that integrates the profit motive with the desire to be global citizens. That is the first part. The next part is the risky one.

Manage the Environment of the Network of Conversations

In September 2000, UPS launched a commercial that got everyone talking about people who merely make proposals and then leave it to other people to do the heavy lifting. Here's how it went:

> Three men sit in a room, one behind a desk, two on the other side. As the commercial opens, their power meeting is visible from outside the glass office. The camera snaps to inside the meeting.
>
> "We think you need to integrate your global supply chain," one of the two men says, "and shift your assembly overseas."
>
> "And accelerate inventory velocity," the other says. Both men lean forward and smile.
>
> The man in the position of power takes a deep breath, summons his courage, and says, "Great! Do it." He smiles with the satisfaction of a commander who has taken decisive action.
>
> The two men look at each other with humorous surprise. One says, "Sir, we don't actually do what we propose."
>
> "We just propose it," adds his colleague.
>
> The commercial shifts to a few seconds of depicting UPS's capability to do what these men could not – and then the scene shows the two men walking out of the lobby. As both pull out cell phones and organizers, one asks the other incredulously, "Do you believe that guy?"

The first question is, why did people find this commercial so funny? Peter Block indirectly addressed this question when he told us: "One of the flaws of management in this day and age is that we fragment accountabilities and then everyone focuses on their own piece." People often see their role as making proposals and leaving the decision making and implementation to others. Often executives see their jobs as making the hard decisions. Both sides get frustrated that the other isn't doing enough. Block suggests, "We need to have working teams and networks thinking broader." Such networks don't care about who is in charge, and they move seamlessly from proposals to implementation.

For new futures to arise, the conversational environment needs to include integrity and future-based communication. For the organizational Self to emerge, people have to take responsibility for the whole of the organization and for the concerns of stakeholders. People have to do more than make proposals. Executives have to do more than make the tough decisions. Everyone has to take ownership for the company, its network of conversations, and the environment in which those conversations take place.

Create Ongoing Conversations with Stakeholders

In *The Corporation*, Sir Mark Moody-Stuart, former chairman of Royal Dutch Shell, tells the following story of a protest at his rural home when he was staying there with his wife. About twenty-five people arrived and hung a banner emblazoned with "Murderers!" They marched around his home in gas masks. In the documentary, Sir Mark says what happened:

> As a public demonstration, it wasn't very effective ... it was a rural area, there were two people and a dog [at home]. ... But then we sat down and talked with them for a couple of hours, gave them tea and coffee, and they had lunch on our lawn.

After about twenty minutes, they said, "Well, the problem's not you, it's Shell." And I said, "Wait a minute, let's talk about what is Shell." It's made up of people like me.

Perhaps the biggest limitation of businesses (not just Shell) is that their network of conversations is managed from the notion "Only involve the people that we *need* to involve," or "Keep the barbarians outside the gates." But somehow the balance between legitimate privacy and appropriate transparency has been lost. As a result, organizations made up of well-intentioned people often commit crimes, oppress local populations, and damage the environment.

Some organizations involve employees in strategic conversations, but they generally don't involve external stakeholders. This, in our view, is a problem and an opportunity—organizations that initiate and engage in ongoing conversations with their external stakeholders will naturally evolve. They will be among the first to build authentic relationships with the groups and communities that they affect.

Returning to the Shell example and Sir Mark's meeting with the protesters, he said, "In the end, what we found in that discussion is all the things that they were worried about, I was worried about, as well. Climate, oppressive regimes, human rights."

There was a big difference between how the situation occurred to Sir Mark and how it occurred to the protesters. In his words: "I feel I can make a contribution to this; these people feel frustrated because they had nothing to do." When stakeholders are not allowed into the network of conversations, they get frustrated and angry, and sometimes they go out of their way to try to shut a company down.

Why doesn't this happen internally in the course of business? The answer is brutally simple. These kinds of conversations threaten management. Block illustrated this when he told us: "I wrote a book on empowerment, and people would bring me in to talk about empowerment, but all they'd really want to talk about was boundaries. I can't give a talk without some manager asking me about anarchy."

Many managers fear that opening up the dialogue to external concerns will mean a total loss of control. Yet there is some logic at work: If an organization does listen to stakeholder concerns and then doesn't follow through in a meaningful way, people will feel let down and angry—worse off than before the process started. The process does require integrity to work—but so does everything else. In our experience, the benefits of a process dedicated to involving external stakeholders far outweighs the risks.

Lonmin is an exception, in part, because of the integrity that has been built into its network of conversations. Its leaders created venues that involved internal and external stakeholders and brought forth the concerns of unions, elected officials, community leaders, workers from all levels, school principals, NGOs, even the World Bank. Sandile Nogxina, the director general of the Department of Minerals and Energy in South Africa, was asked what Lonmin had done differently from other companies. He said, "They listened to us." We add, "and with integrity."

Listen for a Future That Encompasses the Self

An organizational Self emerges when the right seeds have been planted. The conversational environment has to be tended to and implanted with integrity and ownership. The concerns of stakeholders must be an active set of conversations. People have to confront the truth about the default future of the organization and be willing to set it down and to let it go. When all this happens, people begin to glimpse what this group can achieve.

As the Self emerges, people begin to notice that they all have the same vision in mind. Warren Bennis once asked Hollywood director Robert Zemeckis which of his movies he liked the most, and he immediately said, *"Forrest Gump."* "Why?" Bennis asked. Zemeckis said, "We were all making the *same* movie." When an organization is Self-led, as Zemeckis's production crew apparently was, the result is a highly focused and coordinated effort leading to world-class results. And in Zemeckis's case, a slew of Academy Awards.

What if everyone in your company were "making the same movie"? Or striving for the same objective—something important, perhaps difference making?

Oftentimes the Self emerges like a bear jumping out of a cave—suddenly and dramatically. As Lonmin engaged with its communities, it developed a process called the *Lentswe* (which means "voice" in Tswana, one of the six languages spoken in the area). The 150 members of this very diverse group met over a two-year period and developed a charter, vision, and strategic outcomes for the year 2040. As its vision emerged, it startled its authors.

The tipping point for the 150 people occurred when an elderly lady stood up, interrupting an argument over which village would be the first to have streetlights installed, and said:

> The reason nothing gets done around here is that we are all just different villages out for ourselves. We need to get concerned about what will work for everyone. We need to think of ourselves as "The Greater Lonmin Community," not the little villages and communities that we come from.

This birth of the Greater Lonmin Community allowed the participants to experience a new sense of Self, allowing for the future of the local populations to shift from struggle and argument to velocity and creativity.

When their work on the *Lentswe* Charter was done, participants were so moved by it that they produced a video in which *Lentswe* members read, sang, and danced—in South African tradition—about their vision for 2040. When the Self emerges, it's palpable and startling.

Peter Block commented on approaches like this when he said:

> In the future, freedom will become an organizing principle, and will replace control and predictability. The personal transformation movement in the 1970s facilitated people to ask, "This is my life, now what do I want it to be?" Now it's time for people in organizations to say, "This is mine, now what do I want it to be?"

Governments can fuel the emergence of this new kind of corporation by offering incentives to manage for future shareholder value and avoiding excessive externalization.

Don't Lose Your Self

Once the Self of an organization is clear, leaders step forward and use future-based language to make declarations. Managers come forward to build systems, processes, policies, and procedures to turn these declarations into reality.

The Self is potent; it is also easily driven away. In the course of writing this book, we came across several cases in which leaders did everything in this chapter up to this point, and then the effort collapsed. Sometimes it was because the company was sold, and the new management didn't understand what this effort was about. In other cases, a champion of the initiative left the company without training a successor. Without continuity, the Self of an organization dissipates, like smoke on a windy day, allowing politics and short-term interests to take over.

Self-Led Management

Toward the end of our writing project, we met at Steve's home in Miami to review the cases, interviews, and work that spanned almost eight years. One of our biggest supporters in writing this book is a medical doctor turned business consultant, Halee Fischer-Wright. As we discussed why more organizations don't focus on the Self, she commented, "There needs to be a Hippocratic oath of management."

The more we discussed the situation, the more her suggestion seemed perfect. In 1964, Louis Lasagna, academic dean of the School of Medicine at Tufts University, looked at the writings of Hippocrates and crafted the modern version of this oath that is used by most medical schools around the world. Think of the state of modern management as you read what medical doctors commit to. It says, in part:

> I will apply, for the benefit of the sick, all measures [that] are required, avoiding those twin traps of overtreatment and therapeutic nihilism. . . .
>
> I will remember that I do not treat a fever chart, a cancerous growth, but a sick human being, whose illness may affect the person's family and economic stability. . . .
>
> I will remember that I remain a member of society, with special obligations to all my fellow human beings, those sound of mind and body as well as the infirm. . . . May I always act so as to preserve the finest traditions of my calling and may I long experience the joy of healing those who seek my help.

The obvious question is, what would management's version of the Hippocratic oath sound like? We posed this question to a number of academics, business leaders, consultants, famous authors, and other opinion leaders. Most said the current version would say, "I promise to build shareholder value. Period."

One of the experts we interviewed was Rakesh Khurana of the Harvard Business School. In 2007, Khurana wrote *Higher Aims to Hired Hands: The Social Transformation of American Business Schools and the Unfulfilled Promise of Management as a Profession*. At the time we interviewed him, he was finishing work on another book on the need for management to form commitments beyond shareholder value alone.

Like us, Khurana believes in the power of the free enterprise system, but also that management has a lot of work to do. He said, "The original idea [in the twentieth century] was to make management a profession. . . . It didn't happen. The contemporary state of business education is in many ways the antithesis of that idea."

Khurana explained that in the early days of the twentieth century, the public demanded greater accountability of corporations. Congress got involved, and managers promised to self-regulate. He went on: "Management had a *Field of Dreams* approach. . . . 'If we build a business school, the profession will come.'" Business schools became a growth area for universities, but management never found its noble purpose.

Instead, management developed an increasingly potent set of tools to return value to shareholders. Based on the scientific management approach, and newer approaches in the decades that followed, managers learned to create job descriptions, disperse decision rights, set goals, evaluate performance, and coordinate the work of thousands of people. Management focused on the mechanics of achievement, and the results are beyond impressive. As Khurana told us, "The corporation ... lifted more people out of poverty and created more well-being than anything else. But what's been missing is to contextualize the corporation within the society in which it's embedded. We've lost the ability to have discourse to address that ... what's its purpose?"

The questions facing the profession are: Who is able to lead management toward discovering this purpose? Who can do for management what Dr. Louis Lasagna did for medicine? Said differently, who is able to find the Self in management?

If the last few decades are any indication, this effort won't be led by academics, lawmakers, political activists, or the media. Like most innovations in business, it will come from the business world itself.

Only an accomplished business leader, who has built his or her company into a global citizen, would have the legitimacy to take on such a challenge.

It will come, we believe, from people who marshal the power of the Three Laws of Performance.

As we conclude this middle section of the book, here are some questions that will bring the key points of this chapter into your life:

1. To what extent do the leaders in this organization focus on more than profit?
2. In what ways are we "externalizing"?
3. Of all of the people in this organization, who is best equipped to lead an effort to find the organizational Self?
4. What could I do to facilitate this process?
5. If this organization became Self-led, what impact could we make beyond our own boundaries?

Call for Leaders

For the first time in history, finding an organization's Self is more than a good idea; it is a business imperative. A company that listens and responds to all of its stakeholders can construct a business model to form long-term partnerships throughout the global workplace.

We now turn to the third and last part of this book—mastering the game of performance. It addresses what you will encounter if you take on mastering the Three Laws.

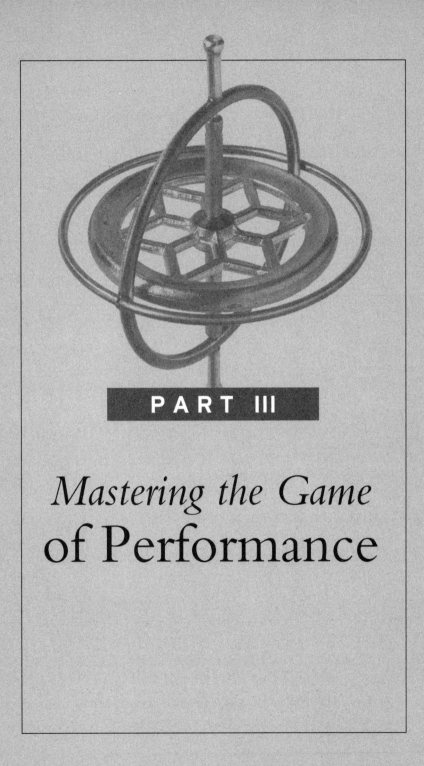

PART III

Mastering the Game
of Performance

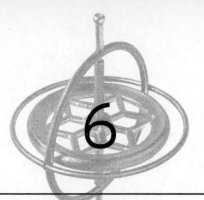

Who or What Is Leading Your Life?

> Everyone thinks of changing the world, but no
> one thinks of changing himself.
> —*Leo Tolstoy*

Who or what is leading your life? The approval of others? Pleasing your mother or father? Others' expectations of you? Proving yourself to others? Maybe proving yourself to yourself?

This chapter is about taking on some deep work—the kind of work that needs to be done for us to be leaders in our lives. And we really mean being a leader in all aspects of our lives, including at work, in relationships, with family, with community, even with all of society. Warren Bennis captures this idea in the first few pages of his self-reflective book, *An Invented Life*. He writes, "I believe in self-invention, have to believe in it. . . . To be authentic is literally to be your own author . . . to discover your native energies and desires, and then find your way of acting on them."

The phrase "native energies and desires," as Bennis uses the words, captures the essence of the best part of a person.

When we build our lives around these, every aspect of our lives transforms.

Here we face a fork in the road—carry on as before, or invent ourselves anew. Most people live a "thrown" life— thrown like dice—finding ourselves caught up in the situations of our lives, but never really calling the shots.

If we take on this challenge of self-invention, we will find ourselves walking down an unfamiliar road. Rather than being led by what has been important to us in the past, we will find ourselves "being" what we are committed to, what we are standing for, what our vision is. We will come across to others as charismatic, wise, self-confident, and at ease in situations. We will be ready for leadership roles in our relationships, groups, organizations, and communities, even society.

This chapter is about what it takes to reinvent ourselves and to be the leader in those areas of our life that matter to us. The required work will include looking at the not-so-pretty pictures of our lives. This exploration will bring up issues that have been hidden from our view or at least issues that we have been putting off resolving.

To repeat a theme from this book, most people have something important that they'll get to "someday." This illusion of "someday" is very pervasive, soothing, and even tranquilizing. But life doesn't fit into this illusion: the daily newspaper offers reports of people dying in car accidents on their way to work. These people didn't wake up expecting that to happen. They were certain that it was just another day at work. Reality can be very rude in its surprises and nasty when it intrudes on our hopes and dreams. Every now and then Lady Luck will smile on someone who wins the lottery, but it never seems to be us.

When we put pictures of our dreams, hopes, and wants into the category of "someday," we separate ourselves from the immediacy of living. Someday never comes. There is only now.

Who Are You, Really?

Colin Wilson, the prolific and influential British writer, was born to working-class parents from a relatively poor community in Britain. Although his ambition was to become the next Albert Einstein, he was forced to quit school at age sixteen.

Working as a laboratory assistant, he fell into despair and decided to end his own life by drinking hydrocyanic acid. In the moment before what was to be his final act, he came to a realization. There were actually *two* Colin Wilsons. It was like two people living in the same body. One was a boy idiot filled with self-pity. The other was his real self.

The boy idiot, he realized, was about to kill them both.

From that moment on, Colin Wilson occurred to himself in a new way. He saw himself as the "real Colin Wilson" instead of the unsuccessful lab technician. He later wrote that from this point, "I glimpsed the marvelous immense richness of reality, extended to distant horizons."

When how a person occurs to himself alters, everything else shifts as well.

Think of the immense job of a leader. Imagine every aspect of her work. This chapter is about building our leadership around our "real" self. Only then will we be ready to lead others, organizations, and even society, to new places.

How Did You Become Who You Are?

There are many models that explain how we became the person we are. See whether this one fits.

We all have defining moments in our lives that set us on the path we're on. Here are two of ours. The first is from Steve:

On the first day of seventh grade, I sat in my classroom, and didn't see any of my friends, but instead saw that the tough kids were my classmates. At lunch, I met up with my friends and asked which class they were in. Some said "7-1." Others said "7-2." I was in 7-3.

It took only a moment for all of us to figure out what the class designations meant. Smart kids went to 7-1. Dumb kids went to 7-3.

Clearly there had been a mistake. I should have been in 7-1.

At the end of the class day, I walked to the door of the school's guidance counselor and knocked. A tall man—very tall, particularly to a seventh grader—pulled back the door, leaning forward to hear my question. I said, "I'm in 7-3 and that must be a mistake. My friends are all in 7-1 or 7-2."

The counselor said, "Do you remember those tests you took at the end of sixth grade?"

"No."

Testing, studying, doing well on homework were items that had not been important to my life. Playing in the courtyard—that was important.

"Those tests determined which class you went into. So no, there was no mistake. You are in the right classroom."

And then he closed the door. I stood there for what seemed an eternity, staring at the door and thinking, *What am I going to tell my mother?* To this day, I can remember the color and pattern of the wood.

After several seconds of staring at the now closed door, I came to a crashing realization: *Something is wrong here, and there is something wrong with me.*

I said to myself, *I'm not smart enough.* This was the kind of news that I had to keep quiet, particularly from my mother. After all, she was counting on me becoming a doctor. Instead of succumbing, not being smart enough, I decided to do something about it—study. Studying had never been a concern of mine—but it was now. The strategy was this—since I wasn't really smart, study, study, and study. Perhaps hard work would make up for not being smart enough.

Partway through the year, the school tested its students on math and English. I scored 100 percent in math and 95 percent in English. I was moved from the 7-3 classroom to 7-1. The kids now thought that I was really smart. But I never really felt that way.

In the privacy of his mind, Steve had fooled them. Under the nagging doubt of *I'm not smart enough,* he kept studying, getting great grades, being in the honor society, standing out from others. But regardless of the academic success he obtained, he could never remove how he occurred to himself: *not smart.* No matter how much he masked his insufficiency through hard work, he occurred to himself as the seventh-grade boy standing in front of the guidance counselor's door. Years later, with a degree from Cornell (with honors) and a master's degree in philosophy from the University of Chicago, the same nagging feeling remained. Steve continues:

When I would go into a new class, I wouldn't say anything until I had assessed that I was at least as smart as some of the others. My freedom to express myself and provide leadership roles in the class was diminished by this nagging doubt.

In all of our lives there are moments when we make critical decisions about ourselves that give us an overriding sense of who we are, not just in the present moment, but from then on. Based on the special self-defining nature of these decisions, we see ourselves in a way that limits who we are and what we can do. For us to find the path to something greater, we first need to see the road that's brought us to this point. Dave Logan's critical decision happened over dinner when he was about eight years old:

I was eating dinner with my parents, who had a startling resemblance to Ward and June Cleaver in *Leave It to Beaver*, with my older brother and sister. We were talking about Ronald Reagan running for president. My liberal father was outraged, my conservative mother was delighted, and a family debate raged over chicken, mashed potatoes, gravy, and broccoli.

In the midst of a heated discussion about whether the world would end, I said in a squeaky voice, "It'll be OK." My sister, who I always thought was brilliant and cool, shot back, "Why don't you just shut up when you don't have anything to say?" Under her breath, she said, "God! You always *do* that!"

Time slowed down as the "truth" settled in. I said to myself: *I always do that . . . I never have anything to say.* And even deeper, I concluded: *There's something wrong with me . . . I must be worthless.*

I wouldn't give up. Scrambling to recover my dignity and my sister's admiration, I said, "Well, my teacher told us that Reagan could get the respect of the Soviets."

After I said that, the most amazing thing happened: everyone actually listened. Even my sister. So I now knew that quoting authorities was a way to make up for my lack of having anything useful to say.

My right to say anything became tied to saying what the experts said.

This view of myself persisted for years, even after I got my Ph.D. In media interviews I would quote the experts instead of saying my own view. My ability to be a thought leader was suppressed. In lieu of having something to say, I was willing to settle for credibility instead of expressing my points of view. The cost was that I had lost my voice.

The decisions that shape our lives live in a conversational environment that includes *There is something wrong here* and *Something is wrong with me.* For Steve, something was wrong about being in a class with the tough, not very smart kids. And something was wrong about him—he wasn't smart enough. For Dave, something was wrong when his cool sister shot him down. And something was wrong about him—he was worthless and had nothing to say.

See if you can recall those pivotal moments when you experienced *something is wrong here,* and *something is wrong with me.* If so, look and see what decision you made to deal with these kinds of situations in the future: a decision specifically about being a certain way, now and in the future, a way you could be that would produce results and make up for what's wrong about you.

The decisions we make that deal with what's wrong about us form the basis of our persona—who we consider ourselves to be.

It's important to realize that these are not ordinary decisions, like which movie to see or where to go for dinner. These kinds of decisions are life altering. It is as if you are at a trial, and the trial are about how well you are dealing with life. You are playing three roles at the same time: the accused, the jury, and the judge. That you are going to find yourself guilty is almost preordained. Otherwise, why is there a trial? Once the evidence is in—that is, once you have reviewed what you said is wrong about you—a sentence is proclaimed. This sentence is the decision you make about how to deal with the future in a way that makes up for what is lacking in who you are. This is a lifelong sentence with no reprieve. These life sentences limit and narrow how you occur to yourself, and even how life occurs to you.

Steve's life sentence was to study hard to make up for not being smart enough. Dave's was to capture what the authorities said, so as to make up for not having anything to say for himself.

The life sentence works exactly according to the design—it helps you survive and gives you a pathway to achieve success. Steve would study with an obsessive work ethic, and Dave would channel research to give insights on whatever problem faced him.

Many leadership development approaches build on the attributes of the persona we created in that moment of stress and survival by virtue of life sentences. But let's take a hard look at this approach. What happens if we build our leadership on top of these life sentences? At best, it's limited and inauthentic, a persona, hiding what we believe to be the real truth about ourselves. Steve wanted to be seen as smart, but whatever he did was on top of not being smart enough. Dave wanted to be seen as having something to say, but whatever he did produce was on top of having nothing to say. See whether the same may be true for you: are you trying to be seen as other than you are?

Look around at people trying to be leaders, in all walks of life. If you look closely, you can see the persona they became in a moment of crisis long ago. You can see the life sentence they imposed on themselves, and often you can get a sense of what it covers over. For example, imagine some people that are (for themselves) shallow, or unpopular, or unattractive, or unlovable. Imagine the kind of compensations that they would have developed: becoming innovative (on top of shallow), stylish (on top of unpopular), hardworking (on top of unattractive), service oriented (on top of unlovable). You can see the glee of having pulled it off, and deep resignation (often in lines on their faces) that it's not real.

One of the consultants in the Lonmin engagement is Larry Pearson. A big 240-pound ex–football player with a master's in social work, he is formidable in presentation, comfortable and easy to be with in reality. He shared with us how his persona developed during the course of his life. As he tells his story, notice the decision he made, the persona he created, and the limitations that came with both:

> I grew up in a pretty tough African-American neighborhood. In junior high school, I was in the locker room. A guy came up to me and put a knife in my throat and said, "If you don't cry we're going to cut you." After thirty minutes, I thought, "The only way I'm going to get out of here is to cry." So I did. I decided, I will never let anyone mess with me again. I will be stronger than they are. I will always find a way out. I will not get trapped again. I'll be smart enough, cunning enough.

Pearson also had a form of dyslexia; as a result, he had trouble reading. After this incident, he decided that he would find a way out of this reading problem without being trapped by depending on others to read for him. "I couldn't read street signs, so I learned to recognize the kids who went to my school, and I followed them. When we were a few blocks away, I was OK." No one knew he couldn't read, not even his teacher or his mother. "When we'd talk through a book in class, I would wait for someone else to go first, because I hadn't read it. I learned to elaborate on what they said, spinning a story, and so no one ever asked if I had read it. I became a quick-talking, inauthentic liar, but I was really good at it. Unfortunately, I didn't have close friends because I can see now that people didn't really trust something about me."

As Larry learned, people are good at "smelling" inauthenticity. Whenever someone picks up on a lack of consistency in what you say and how you say it, it triggers a sense of distrust and a gut feeling that you're not being straight with them. People can even detect the little unconscious movements our bodies make, and though they can't explain what troubles them, they can see that something is off.

Of course, people don't talk about other people's inauthenticities. It is as if there is an unspoken rule: *Don't call me on my crap and I won't call you on yours. But if you call me on mine, I'll call you on yours!* So everyone walks around pretending not to see the obvious.

The fork in the road we spoke about earlier can now be seen as a choice between fitting in and standing out. We are about to take the fork of the road called "standing out," and it's not for people who are committed to comfort. It involves transforming ourselves, altering the very sense of who we are for ourselves. Doing so will allow us to bring forth abilities, capacities, and intentions that will put us in the driver's seat of our lives.

Seeing into the Constraints of Your Life Sentence

Let's do a thought experiment, right now. Reflect on your leadership experience.

In what situations do you see yourself as being most capable of exercising leadership? Add as many situations as you can to this mental list.

In what particular situations do you see yourself as being least capable of exercising leadership? Make another mental list.

Pick a situation in which you pictured yourself as capable. It's probably in line with the persona you invented in a moment of crisis.[16]

Pick a situation in which you pictured yourself as not capable. It's probably a situation in which your persona would be ineffective.

Look back in your life for an incident that was wrong, in which you decided that something was missing or wrong with you. This will likely be when you were young or at least still growing up. Somehow you managed to survive and deal with this "bad" situation by doing something new, something that covered over what was wrong about you.

Can you recall what you decided to do and how you decided to be to deal with this "wrong" situation? See how you sentenced yourself to the life you are now living—having to be a particular way to make up for "something wrong" about you.

The purpose of this exercise is twofold. First, to see the persona you created as clearly as possible—including where it's effective and where it will fail. Second, to begin to experience the life sentence that gave birth to who you are now. You found a way to survive, and in doing so formed who you are today.

Notice, too, that just as there were two Colin Wilsons, there are really two of you. One is the persona. It seeks to survive in a world in which *something is wrong here*, to look good, to fool others—even to fool yourself. It's built on the foundation of your life sentence.

The other person is who you really are, not bound by the persona. But how do we get beyond the limits of our life sentences?

Overturning the Life Sentence

The good news about the life sentence is that you aren't just the accused, the judge, and the jury. You can also be the court of appeals. You can reverse the conviction and release yourself from the prison of limitations. The bad news is that there is serious work to be done.

First, you have to tell the truth about your life sentence and what it is designed to hide. This step requires reexamining the evidence you used against yourself at trial, and in the light of your present-day adulthood, bringing some compassion to the little person who was just trying to deal with life. Only when the complete case is presented to the court of appeals can it be thrown out.

An obstacle is that most people aren't aware that the trial ever happened. We tend to move on and cover over these incidents. They fade into forgetfulness, so that we survive the moment intact. Afterward, we don't remember the decision; we simply say, "This is who I am."

But you can remember what you forgot. It's a matter of bringing the incident from the background to the foreground. If you watch the incident like a movie, you'll often remember the script. Here is a list of questions that will support you in finding the incident to work with and then to uncover the script that led to your life sentence:

1. How do you want people to describe you (for example, smart, funny, articulate)?

2. When did you decide to be this way? Did you have a moment when you realized, *Something's wrong here*? Can you recall a moment when you said to yourself, *Something's wrong here with me*? What happened in that moment?

3. What decision did you make in that moment about how you would act in the future?

4. As in a court case, motive is important. What was your motive—your intent—in making that decision and in forming a persona? Was it to survive? To look good? To avoid looking bad? Or something else?

Notice how this persona or identity developed. It probably felt like you were just accepting reality. But in fact you were actually responding to how that situation occurred to you and how you occurred to yourself. You then created a new role to play in the future. When Steve said to himself, *I'm not smart enough,* he was both imposing an interpretation on the situation and authoring a future for himself. A different interpretation might have been *I didn't take that sixth-grade test seriously* or *I don't test well, but I'm smart in other ways.* When he said to himself, *I'm not smart enough,* he was making a declaration in the form of a decision. When he said to himself, *I will study hard,* he was making another declaration and decision. In these types of declarations, he was creating for much of his adult life. These weren't merely the actions of a child accepting reality, but rather those of a child creating a reality that stuck with him.

Once the life sentence is revealed for what it is—a decision about how to be in the future, albeit made under a moment of stress—you have a choice. Given that any decision is itself an action requiring language, you can renew or revoke it. But until you see the situation for what it is, you don't have a choice to say anything else about who you are.

Some people's decisions are dramatic, as are the incidents that lead to them. Arunaraje Patil, a soft-spoken woman from Mumbai, India, told us of a situation that happened to her later in life:

I was happily married with two children, working making documentaries and feature films. Then my daughter got cancer when she was nine, and despite going to New York for treatment, she died, about a year after diagnosis. Within twenty-four hours of her death, my husband asked me for a divorce, saying he didn't love me.

I became profoundly sad, but resolved to give my son everything—an education, a good life. I decided I was a reject, but I had to hold on for his sake. Inside, I was crying all the time.

Patil's life sentence was that she could never be happy again, given that she had lost her daughter and her husband, both of whom she loved so much. She revisited this incident, and the decision she made, in a Landmark Education course. She told us: "As I went through the program I realized that suffering could be looked at as a choice, and that hit me like a bullet. I realized that I had chosen to suffer for the sake of my son, but that my sadness prevented me from giving him the thing that mattered most—a happy mother." She continues: "My spirit soared. I could laugh. I decided to no longer be a victim of circumstances. It all changed, suddenly and dramatically."

Patil was able to create a new interpretation for her suffering. This new interpretation, although unusual, was one that allowed her to create a future of power, one without suffering. It wasn't an interpretation made up to make her feel good (like positive thinking), but one that both fit the facts and left her with a choice in the matter of her own suffering.

Notice that rewriting her future required future-based (generative) language. Prior to that moment she was using descriptive language, trapped by her situation.

Only when you see that it was you who made these decisions and judgments about and on yourself can you then overturn the life sentence. If you believe another person did it to you, or the circumstances did it to you, then you have no power. But if you are the imposer of the judgment, then you can revoke it.

Extraordinary leadership emerges from the following question: "If I'm not that persona, who am I, really?"

Creating a Crisis of Authenticity

The following story illustrates what we call *creating a crisis*.

> An old Cherokee chief is teaching his grandson about life:
> "A fight is going on inside me," he said to the boy. "It is a terrible fight and it is between two wolves.
> "One is evil—he is anger, envy, sorrow, regret, greed, arrogance, self-pity, guilt, resentment, inferiority, lies, false pride, superiority, self-doubt, and ego.
> "The other is good—he is joy, peace, love, hope, serenity, humility, kindness, benevolence, empathy, generosity, truth, compassion, and faith.
> "This same fight is going on inside you—and inside every other person, too."
> The grandson thought about it for a minute and then asked his grandfather, "Which wolf will win?"
> The old chief simply replied, "The one you feed."

This notion is different from how we think of crises, which are usually circumstantial. Lose a job, survive a tornado, get a diagnosis of a life-threatening illness—these are crises of circumstance.

We aren't referring to a crisis you *have*, but a crisis you *create*, by confronting what really matters to you. It's a crisis of the real you against the persona and the life sentence.

Or, in the words of the Cherokee chief, between "anger, envy, sorrow, regret ..." and "joy, peace, love, hope, serenity."

The idea of intentionally creating a crisis is counterintuitive. Who wants a crisis? Isn't life about avoiding crises? Isn't life about fun and going to the beach? But if you want to transform who you are—how you occur to yourself—then you need to create a crisis of identity, one in which the only way out is transformation.

To return to an earlier theme, consider your life a three-act play. The life sentence happened early in the first act, followed by hard work and success, but with a nagging realization that it's not fulfilling. Imagine a third act in which the life sentence has been reversed, and you have your life renewed, free of resignation, regret, and pretense.

In the last one hundred years, many scholars have studied the stories we love to hear and tell. From *The Odyssey* to *Long Day's Journey into Night* to *Hamlet* to *Star Wars* to *Gone with the Wind*, every major story follows a similar path. There is action, complication, crisis, climax, reversal, and resolution. The secret to rewriting your play is a crisis of your own creation. From that flows climax, reversal, and resolution.

How do we create this kind of crisis that moves us into transforming ourselves? We do it by focusing on the areas of our lives in which we are inauthentic, those times when we are pretending. Inevitably, these are the areas of our lives in which we have resigned ourselves to a lack of freedom, joy, and full self-expression. We create a crisis by giving up the resignation and standing for a life in which we experience being ourselves, fulfilled and empowered.

In the 1970s, a man took a program Steve was leading. On the first day, he stood up and said: "I was in a concentration camp thirty years ago. I got out, moved here to New York, but

I never really got out. Every day I wake up with anger and resentment for the guards, what they did to me and my family, friends, and their fellow human beings."

He asked, "Can I somehow get free, get out of the camp?" Steve tells the story of what happened next:

I said, "You can, but you're not going to like what I tell you is the way out."

"What's the way out?"

I responded: "Forgiveness. That's your way out."

The man was very upset. He shouted, "No way! They killed my family!"

I really felt this person's horror and his turmoil. It was beyond anything I had experienced before. I had enormous compassion, but I still had to deal with his request for freedom. "I said you wouldn't like what I told you. But look at what your anger and resentment is costing you. You live with it every day. I am not talking about what you *should* do. I'm only responding to your question about how to get out of the concentration camp. You are obviously free to do whatever works for you.

"If you could find a way to bring forgiveness to what happened—and I do know that what happened was ugly, brutal, senseless, crazy—then you would be free."

I added: "I didn't say 'condone' what happened. There is no way what happened can be condoned. I did say 'forgive.' To forgive is to give up resentment. It can be a blow for freedom."

The man sat down, crossed his arms, and didn't say a word for the next three days of the program.

On the last day of the program, he walked in with a radiance and light that was startling.

He said: "I've been dealing with what you said all week. I thought back to those days in the camp and looked at the people involved. I also looked at my life and the trap I've been in. I realized that if I could get out of this trap, it was worth examining my views, my certainties about the way things are. I saw that I could authentically create another interpretation of the people and the times. I could see my captors as people were as lost and dominated and frightened as we were, only they had the guns.

"That doesn't excuse them. But remaining their 'victim' forty years later is not worth my life. It doesn't give me any satisfaction. I forgive them. Let them deal with their own demons. I'm not willing to live my life in the space of guilt and resentment."

He actually smiled and sat down.

In a short period of time, this man created and then resolved a crisis that turned his life in a new direction, from a default future to something else. If he can do it, with all he suffered, I realized that anyone can.

To create your crisis, you need to locate where your foot is nailed to the floor. Here are some questions that can support you in creating a crisis of identity in which the only way out is transformation:

- Where in your life is something not working or not working as well as you want?
- In what areas of your life do you feel a loss of power, freedom, fulfillment, or self-expression?

Consider that wherever you experience a loss of quality in your life, there is some inauthenticity at play. Simply said, there is something about which you are pretending, avoiding, something you are not taking responsibility for. Or you've made a decision that makes you right, that gives you justification. In doing so, you give up power, freedom, and self-expression. We hide from others and even from ourselves the game we are playing. This self-deception is at the heart of the trap.

1. In those areas of life you just identified, how are you being inauthentic—what are you pretending, avoiding, not taking responsibility for?

2. What can you see has been the impact, the limitations, of your having been inauthentic in those areas?

The purpose of the life sentence is to produce results through making up for what is wrong with you. But it hides from others and even from yourself who you are afraid you are. It has you pretending that you are different from who you think you are. It even has you pretending that you aren't pretending. This is what the crisis calls you to face.

The way out of the trap is to create a crisis over *being in the trap*. Tolerating any loss of freedom, power, contentment, self-expression becomes unacceptable.

To resolve the crisis, you will have to give something up.

What Do You Have to Give Up?

In their book *Fox on the Rhine*, Douglas Niles and Michael Dobson[17] tell a story about Mark Twain:

It seems that Mark Twain caught pneumonia. When the doctor visited, he saw Mark Twain smoking a cigar. He asked, "How many of those do you smoke each day?" Twain said, "Oh, about a dozen or so." And the doctor said, "I see a bottle of whiskey. How much do you drink?" Twain said, "I'm a moderate drinker, only a bottle or so a day." The doctor said, "If you'll temporarily give up drinking and smoking, you'll recover quickly." Twain followed the doctor's advice, and got well. Later, a woman he knew got pneumonia and Twain told her that if she temporarily stopped drinking whiskey and smoking cigars, she'd get well.

She said, "I don't drink whiskey, and I don't smoke cigars."
And you know, she died.

Mark Twain's conclusion was that his friend died because she didn't have anything to give up.

Every life sentence carries a benefit. Otherwise, it wouldn't have the hold that it has. As the Cherokee chief said, the "evil" wolf is alive because you're feeding it. Consider that we feed only what we value.

What there is to give up is the certainty you obtain from the life sentence. The life sentence does provide a reliable way to deal with the risk of life. It may be limiting your quality of your life, but at least it seems to work.

Consider the following story from Eraldo Tinoco in Brazil:

> I was about sixteen years old, and I lived in a neighborhood where some families had a lot of money and others didn't. Mine didn't. In fact, we were one of the poorest families there.
>
> I had to start work at an early age, delivering telegrams. The position required that I wear a uniform with a hat, and every time I left the office I had to have the hat on. I had the feeling that everyone in the neighborhood was looking at me.
>
> One day, I delivered a telegram to a lady and she asked if she could have the information about my hat, so she could get one for her daughter to wear for Carnival.
>
> I told her to take the hat and I would come back and get it later.
>
> In that moment, I felt on display, alone, isolated, and different from people my age. I decided to become someone worthy of respect—someone who would work hard for the poor.
>
> I never went back to get the hat.

Throughout his career, he did work hard, earning a doctorate, entering politics, and becoming the secretary of education and, later, vice governor for Brazil's state of Bahia. But the life sentence he imposed on himself exacted a price. Wanting to never be alone or different, he would make only safe decisions. He would hand off risky decisions to others, so his ability to make an impact was lessened. He lived in fear of being revealed as the person who was different, alone, and isolated.

In 2001, Tinoco told the story to people he worked with, including the part about the hat. He resolved to give up the life sentence and instead fashion his life around quality education for everyone, no matter the risk or how much he'd have to act alone—at least at the start.

In the years that followed, until his death in 2008, Tinoco started several bold projects that required his personal leadership. He did so without the anxiety and "safety" that were part of his life sentence. Today, he is known for instituting the certification of school principals in Bahia, ensuring a greater quality of education for everyone.

When he told us the story shortly before his death, he added: "One of the people who heard my story went to a local store, bought me a hat. He had it stitched with the name of the project I was leading. Today I have this hat, and prize it deeply."

To experience the kind of transformation that we point to here—overturning your already-written future and writing it anew—there's one last matter that needs to be addressed: What are you willing to give up? Tinoco had to give up safety and risk avoidance. Pearson had to let go of always having a way out. Dave had to give up the fear of having nothing to say. Steve had to give up the fear of saying something stupid.

Bringing It Home

A fallout for people and organizations using applications derived from the Three Laws of Performance is an improved quality of life for employees and people in surrounding communities. One story illustrates the point.

When Magma Copper first acquired its Peruvian Tintaya copper mine, the operation was a fortified camp with private guards carrying AK-47s. Adjacent to the mine was the community of the workers' wives and children.

The rate of drug and spousal abuse was so high that the total population of four thousand people needed a hospital with three full-time doctors and five nurses. Within two years of applying new processes derived from the Three Laws, the drug and spousal abuse had decreased by almost 90 percent, allowing the hospital staff to decrease to one doctor and two nurses.

The change in behavior of the workers was so dramatic that a number of their wives requested a "town meeting" where they could find out what was going on with their husbands. The first meeting took place in the local movie theater. Eight hundred employees, wives, and children attended. Dogs ran around looking for dropped cookies or other nibbles.

The president of the mine, Lee Browne, along with the two presidents of the local unions, started the meeting, but they were soon interrupted by a woman who demanded to speak. She said, "What have you done to my husband?" Before anyone could answer, she went on, "He came home last night and took the garbage out. He never did that before." She paused and smiled. "I actually don't care what you did to him—I just want you to do it to me."

So many people made the same request that the company sponsored a program for nonemployees, including spouses and teenagers.

The point is that applications derived from the Three Laws of Performance can take companies to that elusive next level. Equally significant, they can take people's personal lives to a level of effectiveness that many didn't think was possible.

Who Gives You the Right?

During work with Reebok in Japan, Steve noticed something odd. He tells the story:

> As we neared the end of the initial program, we were creating the conversational environment in which the Reebok employees could create a new Third Act for their work. We distinguished the nature of future-based language, and the power of declarations, commitments, and promises.
>
> I invited people to write down what they were committing to and were promising to do as leaders for the future of Reebok in Japan. As people wrote, some raised their hand and asked, through the translator, if they could share what they were writing. As one after another rose to speak, I was surprised by how long it took them to convey a commitment or promise.
>
> I asked Ueda-san, my translator, "Why is the English way of saying a commitment so short and the Japanese translation so long?"
>
> She said, well, "We don't really have a simple way of saying future-based language in Japanese."
>
> I pressed on because the whole thing didn't make sense. I wondered, *How could a society as successful as the Japanese not have a way of making declarations, commitments, and promises?* I asked Ueda-san to tell me what people were literally saying, word for word.
>
> As the next person spoke, she translated: "From here on and into the future, I would very much like to be proactive in communicating with my colleagues at work."

This was an expression of a wish, a hope, something to be desired, some way to become. The person was not coming from "This is the way it is because I say so."

In what was perhaps a moment of insight pushed along by exasperation, I asked, "Who here tells people the way it is because they say so?"

People lightened up. One person shouted out, "The shogun, of course. If he says 'it's a good day to die,' it is."

I got it. In the Japanese culture, the right to call it the way it is was relegated to the authority, the shogun, the boss. That person had the authority and therefore the power to make declarations.

I said, "In this part of the program, you now need to use the language of the shogun. Are you willing to be the shogun in your own life?"

Immediately someone stood up and said, "Here I declare, I am someone who communicates new possibilities." His tone was short, focused, and powerful. He spoke as if it mattered.

This shift in power spread through all the participants. One after another, they spoke in a new way: short, powerful, declarative.

This issue of the right to declare is not an issue just in Japanese society. It plays itself out in other cultures in different ways. The underlying theme is, Who are you to make declarations about the future? Who gives you the right?

Ultimately, you need to be willing to appoint yourself the shogun in your own life. If you don't, you turn that power over to others and to your circumstances.

Let's return to the moment of your life sentence, the moment when you experienced that *something's wrong here*. You will see that you, not others, authored who you are. The power is in what you *said* about what happened, not in what happened. In this reexamination of your self and your life, you can use the same power of language that you used as a child to create a new person, unconstrained by the limits of the past. As an adult who is not trying to survive something but who is inventing a life, you can be guided by wisdom.

While in Japan to update our research, we met with some of the executives of the Polus Group. Dave tells the story about what happened:

> The man said: "Early in my life, I decided that I would be the one to make decisions, because I could only rely on myself. That didn't work so well when I got married." (Here he laughed.)
>
> "We recently bought a house, and I wasn't letting her decide anything. It was stressful for her, because she was going to be there most of the time while I would go to work. I remembered that in the work Steve did with us. I declared, like the shogun, that I was one who listens. So I listened, and it was hard because it was like there was a battle in me between the person who decides and the commitment I made to listen.
>
> "In the end, I listened." He laughed, "And she became a better wife!"
>
> Steve said, "I think you are saying that you listened, and just by listening, she occurred to you in a new way."
>
> He added: "Yes, she occurred as a partner."
>
> Steve said, "I'll bet that you also experience yourself differently."
>
> The senior executive from Japan, who rarely showed emotion, paused, wiped a tear away, and said with a deep nod, "Yes."
>
> While I was an administrator at USC, I represented the university in several dealings with Japanese companies and with the government. I never saw that kind of authentic vulnerability, or that level of respect, shown to someone who wasn't Japanese. As I watched the interaction, and heard the

English version through our translator, I felt touched by our common humanity.

When we alter how we occur to ourselves, everything around us shifts. Our business associates, our families, even life, show up in a new way. With that new foundation, anything is possible—even a new future.

The Path to Mastery

Jacques Derrida once wrote, "If things were simple, word would have gotten around." There are many reasons why gains in performance remain elusive, despite the good intentions of very smart people. One of the reasons is that our culture seeks out simple answers, sound bites, steps, tips, and techniques. This desire is illustrated when someone asks in a training session, "How can I use this tomorrow?"

To push this illustration to the point of absurdity: imagine if medical students asked that question, especially those seeking a complex specialty like neurosurgery. "So we've spent an hour learning about the blood supply to the brain and spine. How can we use this on patients starting tomorrow?"

Disciplines require significant work before they become useful—brain surgery and elevating performance being two examples. In fact, the more work that's required, the greater the reward for those willing to make the investment.

This chapter is about mastering the Three Laws, which means being able to achieve levels of performance in your life and business that occur as impossible to most people.

Personal mastery of any discipline or art appeals to those who desire to move beyond mere competence to a position of power, freedom, peace of mind, and full self-expression. Consider what masters in different fields can do that the rest of us can't, and consider how the experience occurs to them.

A grand master at chess has the power, freedom, and peace of mind to play fifty boards at the same time. He walks to one, looks at the board, and the winning move is obvious to him. He moves a piece and walks on. After an hour, he's not only won all fifty games but also enjoys the expression of his prowess.

Richard Feynman was a master physicist. Long before he won the Nobel Prize in 1965 for his work on quantum electrodynamics, he was a junior member of the Manhattan Project. Feynman was sought out by Niels Bohr, perhaps the greatest of the physics minds on that project, to have a one-on-one discussion about the theoretical nature of the group's work. Why did Bohr choose a junior member? Because Feynman was a master physicist in the making—and Bohr recognized Feynman's flowering mastery. Most physicists were too in awe of Bohr to argue with him. Feynman said he felt as much respect for Bohr as anyone else, but he experienced no inhibitions in pointing out anything he considered to be flawed in Bohr's thinking. The other physicists tried to strategize in their conversations with Bohr—evidencing their uncertainty. Feynman, as a master, was able to dance.

When a master takes the stage, people stop what they are doing to watch. They know something may happen that people will talk about for years. Masters like Tiger Woods, Garry Kasparov, or Yo-Yo Ma do what occurs as impossible, yet the masters in their fields are not surprised by their performance. For them, it is a self-expression.

The X-Factor in Mastery

The ordinary explanation for what makes someone a master of a discipline or art is that he or she was born with "natural talent." Basketball players are tall, chess players are smart, and runners are fast—and were so from early childhood. But if the road to mastering a subject is reducible to some physical or mental attributes, why aren't there many more people who can play golf like Tiger, chess like Kasparov, or the cello like Yo-Yo Ma, or do physics like Feynman? And why are there the counter-examples of extraordinary people who seem ordinary or even disabled? As evidence that being born with talent doesn't explain mastery, consider that Winston Churchill mastered oratory yet stuttered from childhood and suffered from what he called the "black dog" of depression. Helen Keller, known for her writing and lecturing, lost her hearing and sight as an infant.

Many people born with advantages, even those who seriously practice their discipline, don't achieve their potential greatness. What is it that explains the elevated performance of some and the lack of mastery in others? More important, how can you use whatever this "x-factor" is to take your performance to a new level?

We assert that the x-factor is the way in which situations occur to the masters of their fields. The way in which the circumstances occur to a master makes the master's performance possible, reliable, and consistently superior to that of other people. This same insight allows us to see what it will take to master the Three Laws of Performance themselves.

To get a glimpse into the experience of mastery, note that each of the masters we've discussed thinks *from* the principles of their field. This is very different than thinking *about* the principles. Richard Feynman thought *from* the laws of physics, therefore things occurred to him as possible that struck others as hard, complex, or impossible. Feynman's commitment to being at the source of whatever he worked on is illustrated by the following story: While on vacation as a teenager, he forgot a reference book on geometry, which provided the proofs of theorems. Starting with the basic axioms, which he remembered, he set out to prove the theorems on his own. When he returned home, he realized that many of his proofs were actually better than those in the book he had neglected to take with him. He brought this approach to his work in physics. Until his death, he could create all the major laws of physics by thinking from basic axioms, and this way of thinking gave him an advantage in performance. He once complained that his CalTech students couldn't do physics the way he did physics. They didn't have his insights and hunches. They thought *about* the laws of the field, not *from* them. On his blackboard at CalTech, written shortly before his death, is the statement: "What I cannot create, I do not understand."

The essence of mastering any discipline or set of new ideas is approaching the new ideas without preconceptions, seeing them for what they are by themselves, and then creating from them. For an example of the power of seeing something on its own terms, consider Wilbur Smith's description, in his book *River God*, of a scholar in ancient Egypt who sees a wheel for the first time—part of an army of attacking chariots:

> the leading vehicle ... moved on spinning discs, and I stared at it in wonder. For the first few moments I was so stunned by what I was looking at that my mind refused to absorb it all. If anything, my first sight of a chariot was almost as moving as the

horses that drew it. There was a long yoke-pole between the galloping pair, connected to what I later came to know as the axle. . . .

All this I took in at a glance, and then my whole attention focused on the spinning discs on which the chariot sailed so smoothly and swiftly over the rough ground. For a thousand years we Egyptians had been the most cultured and civilized men on earth; in the sciences and the religions we had far outstripped all other nations. However, in all our learning and wisdom we had conceived nothing like this. Our sledges churned the earth on wooden runners that dissipated the strength of the oxen that dragged them, or we hauled great blocks of stone over wooden rollers without taking the next logical step. I stared at the first wheel I had ever seen, and the simplicity and the beauty of it burst in upon me like lightning flaring in my head. I understood it instantly, and scorned myself for not having discovered it of my own accord. It was genius of the highest order, and now I realized that we stood to be destroyed by this wonderful invention.[18]

The moment the scholar grasped a wheel on its own terms—saw the situation in terms of the principles of circular motion—he could create one.

The rest of this chapter is in two parts. First, we'll examine what you can expect on the path to mastery of the Three Laws, starting with the fact that there are no steps, tips, or rules along the way. As with anyone walking a path, you need to make sure you stay on course, and just as with any path, there are milestones you'll pass.

Second, we will jump into some questions, which are designed to pull you into a full grasp of the Laws of Performance. As you deal with these questions, your journey begins, and you'll notice yourself making progress as you pass the milestones we discuss in the first part.

In addition to passing the milestones, there is another important sign of progress: your ability to impact performance will move to another level. As the milestones section explains, this increase in abilities is subtle. You will find yourself doing things that occurred to you as impossible before. You won't have to remember to take these actions; you'll simply do them. It's as though a new intuitive ability has taken over, one you didn't have before.

Why There Are No Steps to Mastery

Mastering the Three Laws is like learning French. You start by learning words and translating them to your English words. It's slow and annoying.

The way to really learn the language is by immersing yourself in it—by moving to Paris. Bit by bit, things click. In time, words and phrases begin to make sense. You can order food in French and get what you actually ordered. You begin to think in French, even dream in it. You see things from a new perspective. As linguists have pointed out, there are phrases, thoughts, and ideas that can be said in one language and not in another. One of the benefits of learning a new language is being able to think and say thoughts that were impossible before.

Thinking about this analogy gives us insights. Although immersion in French isn't linear, there are key milestones you'll pass as you become fluent.

We now turn to the first milestone on the road to mastery of the Three Laws: seeing that these laws are a counterintuitive way of approaching situations.

Milestone 1: Seeing Your "Terministic Screen" in Action

Before we get to the experience of this first milestone on the path to mastery, we have to do a bit of background work.

A person's way of seeing a situation is filtered through what scholar Kenneth Burke calls a "terministic screen." This screen itself is made up of language—words, terms, phrases, and their relation to each other. This screen directs our attention to aspects of reality.[19] We don't see the world, and we don't see the terministic screen; instead, we see what the screen allows us to see.

It's like seeing the world through a pair of contact lenses. After we adjust to their newness, we aren't aware of how they modify our vision, and we don't stop to think about what objects we could see clearly without them. There's just the world, and our lenses, merged into a single image. So it is with a screen of terms. We don't see the screen. We don't see the world. We see the world through the screen. And just as with contact lenses, we forget the screen is there.

To picture a terministic screen in action, imagine how a physician sees a patient. She sees illness, patient history, probable diagnoses, causes to rule in or out, and likely courses of treatment. She is looking at the patient through the vocabulary and principles of medicine, intuiting the condition of the patient and arriving at a diagnosis.

Notice that the doctor doesn't have to think about her terministic screen. It's simply there, doing its work, invisibly—like the pair of contact lenses. As a result of the screen, conclusions and actions appear obvious.

Consider how a business occurs to a person with an MBA. He sees profit and loss, expenses, compensation, market positioning, competitors, strategy, and reporting relation-ships. These factors are so obvious to him that he can't *not* see them.

Dave teaches in a Marshall School of Business master's degree program for physicians. He describes teaching doctors the terministic screen of business:

> At first, the doctors hear words that they recognize: *profit*, *cash*, *operations*, and *leadership*. We all know those words, and we think we know what they mean. But in business school, we use these words very precisely, and often they don't mean what they mean to a layperson. The physicians—all smart, accomplished people—learn more and more terms in marathon sessions, going eight to twelve hours a days. The doctors often become stressed, having to get up and get coffee, or stand at the back and stretch. What's happening behind the scenes, in their minds, is that we're stretching their terministic screen to the breaking point. We're adding terms that don't fit to what they already know. The stress is that they understand new terms through an increasingly complex set of connections to older terms, resulting in frustration and a sense of mental disorganization.

The magic moment comes at different points for different people, but it's usually when we're talking about leadership.

Leadership is about inventing something radically new, in concert with those who will implement it, and it can't be done through a formula, steps, or a checklist. The doctors get increasingly uncomfortable—their terministic screen, as physicians, is almost all formulas, steps, and checklists. So if leadership isn't those things, what is it? It sounds like mumbo jumbo. It's literally a thought they can't hold in their head, because it doesn't tie to anything else they know as physicians.

There's an "Aha!" moment when it clicks, and they give in to the demands of the new terms. The moment is dynamic and transformative. It's as though they suddenly put in new contact lenses, understanding new terms in relation to other new terms. Soon they can speak the new language of leadership as well as their older language of medicine, and they know when to pull up the appropriate screen. They look back at their frustration from a few days before and laugh. On the other side of the "Aha!" it all appears simple and obvious.

This struggle is more than just using new words in new ways. As a screen is replaced with another, the same situation looks completely different. As Kenneth Burke wrote, "A way of seeing is also a way of not seeing." When we replace one terministic screen with another, we see things we couldn't see before, and our actions correlate. If we alter the screen, the way the world occurs, shifts. It is a transformation in the truest sense. Old situations occur in a new way.

Dave often speaks to prospective MBA students. Here is how he describes the process of talking with them:

> People often ask me, "What will I learn in a great MBA program?" Part of the answer is what people want to hear. You'll learn tools: accounting, financial, operational, managerial, and so on. But you can learn those tools in a book or through Internet videos. What's more, you can hire people who have those tools. The real value of a great MBA program isn't the tools, but that you leave the program seeing the world as a leader and general manager.
>
> What I don't say to the prospective students, but am thinking, is that we do our best to impart the terministic screen of a business leader into each graduate. They don't need to remember to use that terministic screen, it's just there. Through that terministic screen, they see opportunities where others see

chaos. They see system failures and possible fixes while others only complain that things aren't working. Because they see the world through a terministic screen others don't have, they do things others can't do, or wouldn't imagine doing.

Because we can't see our terministic screen—just like we can't see contact lenses when they're on our eyeballs— we aren't aware of the mechanism at work.

The MBA student often can't explain why the program was so valuable; he can only say that it was. The doctor returning to her hospital can't explain the "Aha!" moment in a way that conveys the insight to others. She can only describe it, and when she does, it may seem trite to people who didn't go through it themselves. Try explaining to a child how to ride a bike. Your advice will fall on deaf ears—and certainly won't have the child riding the bicycle. But after he "gets it" and rides the bicycle, he may say, "Now I see what you were saying!"

The path to mastering the Three Laws is to build a new terministic screen around new core distinctions. To do this, it's helpful to see how a terministic screen works, so we can catch ourselves when we're understanding the Three Laws in terms of what we already know.

In a screen, each term fits with the other terms around it, not unlike a wall of bricks. Like bricks that don't quite fit perfectly into the wall, a term here or there may not fit snugly, but it is, at the least, allowed for by the placement of other terms around it. When we are presented with anything new—such as a new word in a language we don't speak, or an idea in a field we haven't learned—we immediately search to find a way to link it to terms we know. So we're more likely to say, "Oh, that's just like . . ." or "Well, really, that's no different from..." Someone learning French will sometimes stumble over idiomatic phrases, finding them hard to remember, because they don't translate literally. Her first attempts amount to fitting French words into an English terministic screen, by flipping through a translation book as fast as she can. During the process, she links French words to English terms. The result is like the physicians learning business. They get stressed. It's mentally exhausting. It doesn't feel effortless.

From this perspective, the process of learning something new can be seen to involve fitting what is new with what we knew before as a way of understanding. When we learn in this manner, our terministic screen keeps growing, but always in a self-consistent way. This method of learning works well, provided our terministic screen gives us a foundation that is compatible with what we're learning.

But if we intend to learn something radically new, at some point we will confront the fact that the normal learning process gets in our way. Until we reach that point, we often make adjustments to new ideas by making them fit within our screen. We may say, "I see—this idea is much like x, y, and z..." or "this idea follows from x and y," or "this idea is different from x but not from z...." The result is an alteration of the new ideas to make them consistent with our existing terms. Although the process makes learning easier, it dramatically lessens the potential impact of the new ideas. When you realize that you want to get the full impact of the new ideas, it's time to build a new terministic screen.

This realization is the first milestone: its point is that we allow a new screen to be built by rejecting the need to fit new terms into our already existing screen. We catch ourselves reshaping a new idea to fit what we already know, or rejecting a new idea as being inconsistent with our screen. There's nothing wrong with doing so—it's what happens until we get to the second milestone. Every time we catch ourselves doing this, we can recommit to learning the new material on its own terms—moving ourselves more quickly to the second milestone.

Milestone 2: Building a New Terministic Screen

If the new idea is truly difference making, it opens up new and uncharted territory, as the wheel did for the man in ancient Egypt. If he had linked it to what he already knew—blocks used to build the pyramids and sledges used to drag materials around—he wouldn't have grasped it. The closest we can come in English to what we mean is *getting it*, as in "getting a joke." If you need the joke explained to you, it won't be funny and you certainly didn't get it.

Robert Heinlein faced this limitation in English when he wrote *Stranger in a Strange Land*; he invented the verb *grok*, which means to "grasp, apprehend, or get something completely." The process at play is that the person sees the world through the lens of the new idea.

To see the need to build a new terministic screen, consider how the earth appeared to people for millennia: at the center of the universe, with the sun, moon, and stars moving around it. The sun rises in the east, streaks across the sky, and sets in the west. *Sunrise* and *sunset* are terms built into our language, as shorthand expressions of our observations. It's plain common sense—you can observe it. If you climb a tall mountain to a point where the view of the sun is unobstructed, in the morning you'll see the sun "rise" and in the evening you'll see it "set." The terministic screen on this subject was consistent and compelling. Galileo, in the tradition of Copernicus, argued for a radical new idea that didn't fit into the terministic screen of the day—that it was the earth that did the moving. People responded violently to this theory, which to them clearly was wrong. Some even understood the science behind it, but they still couldn't see themselves as living on a moving sphere. They had understood, but didn't *grok*. Notice also how these new ideas were initially received. Galileo was called in for a little chat with the authorities, which did not go well.

So why is it so easy for us today to "see" ourselves moving around the sun, seeing the universe that Galileo saw? Because we learned a terministic screen with these ideas at the center. Because of our screen, we have no problem imagining asteroids, other worlds, space flight, and life on Mars. All these thoughts would be *impossible* for someone with the old terministic screen.

In their book *On Intelligence*, Jeff Hawkins and Sandra Blakeslee show the power of building a new terministic screen, rather than forcing new ideas into an old model, in their description of how Albert Einstein dealt with the theory of relativity:

> According to rumour, Albert Einstein once said that conceiving the theory of special relativity was straightforward, almost easy. It followed naturally from a single observation: that the speed of light is constant to all observers even if the observers are moving at different speeds. This is counterintuitive. . . . He methodically thought about all the implications of a constant speed of light, and he was led to the even more bizarre predictions of special relativity, such as time slowing down as you move faster, and energy and mass being fundamentally the same thing. Books on relativity walk through his line of reasoning with everyday examples of trains, bullets, flashing lights, and so forth. The theory isn't hard, but it is definitely counterintuitive.[20]

Einstein approached the observation of the unvarying nature of the speed of light as a set of new ideas that needed to be unconcealed, and when he did, he found it easy to build a new terministic screen around it. Scientists who attempted to force the new ideas into an old terministic screen went to their deaths without ever grokking it.

There will come a point, on your road to mastery of the Three Laws, where you will begin to see key points of the laws in terms of other parts of the laws. You may experience that "Aha!" moment when it clicks. At this point, you are building a new terministic screen, from the Three Laws up. This is a critical point on your path to mastering the material in this book.

Milestone 3: You'll See New Opportunities for Elevated Performance Everywhere

Shortly after you pass the second milestone, you'll notice that you are seeing old situations with a new perspective—as though you have new contact lenses in your eyes. You'll be going through the grocery store line and wondering, *How must the situations be occurring to the people here, such that they are doing what they are doing?*

You may find yourself asking deep questions about yourself, such as *How does my spouse occur to me, and me to her, such that we behave as we do?* You may even play with the question *How must I occur to myself, given what I do in these types of situations?*

Many people moving through the ideas, processes, and exercises in this book find that they begin listening in new ways. For those who are looking at situations from the perspective of the Three Laws, knowing how the situation occurs to the other person is more critical than what you think about the situation. For example, you may find yourself asking the other person "How does this situation look to you?" rather than assuming that you know. Or, you may find yourself saying, "The way this situation appears to me ..." in place of stating "how it is" to any rational person. You will see the reality illusion for what it is.

Notice that all of these insights are from the First Law.

From the Second Law, you may begin to observe how people's use of language expresses, sustains, and holds in place the way in which situations occur to them. You may see that people talk in terms of "problems," and things that "went wrong," and "are hard." You'll notice that this is how the situations really *are* for people. They don't occur to them as occurring, they occur as "how it is." The reality illusion is in place.

You may become aware of people's terministic screens. You'll hear the screens at play behind their speaking: artistic screens, business screens, scientific screens, analytical screens, even cultural and regional screens. You'll see the terministic screen people use when they talk about themselves, or relationships, or the future. You'll notice that you can gain relatedness and influence by talking to the terministic screen of others.

You'll become aware that most people talk about the future in terms of the past. You'll notice their default future, often unarticulated, and how their actions correlate with it.

You may sit in a restaurant and look around, asking yourself, *What are people not saying and yet are communicating?* You may find you have new insight into people and why they are doing what they are doing.

From the Third Law, you'll see that some (but really only a few) people talk generatively. Instead of merely describing, they use language to create new futures. You may notice that they're using future-based language, grounded in declarations and commitments. You'll see those rare individuals who listen for the future of their organizations, families, or groups to arise.

You may resolve, and declare, that you are such a person.

A great side benefit of taking the path to mastering the Three Laws is developing leadership, and even charisma. You'll find yourself standing for a future rather than trying to figure one out.

As you declare the future—incorporating the concerns of others—people become engaged, excited, inspired. Workplaces transform. Performance elevates. The default future is rewritten.

You won't have to remember to take actions like those of Malcolm Burns or Brad Mills. You'll do what they did, appropriate to your situation—because they were thinking from the Three Laws, just as you are thinking from the Three Laws.

When facing a performance challenge, you will find yourself asking both yourself and others, "How do situations occur to me and others, such that we are performing the way we are?"

You'll ask, "What conversations need to be completed, and what conversations need to be created, that would alter how these situations occur to the people involved?"

You'll find that you're probing the default future of yourself and others, asking, "Is this what we want? And if not, what *do* we want?"

You will notice that where there used to be a lot of confusion and anxiety about what to do, there now is a clarity and focus for what needs to be created. It's as if the frenzy concerning what could go wrong is replaced with an excitement of what can be created.

Great masters approach their work as a game worth playing: there is passion, intensity, and joy of play.

This third milestone of seeing opportunities for elevated performance everywhere is correlated to realizing that you are no longer remembering the Three Laws. They are now a part of your terministic screen. It's as though they use them rather than you use them. Thinking from the Three Laws will have become as natural as finding your car keys before driving to work.

Milestone 4: Teaching Others

Achieving the last milestone is the subject of the next and final chapter: making the application of the Three Laws a community effort. Simply put, the fourth milestone is itself a means of access to ever-expanding mastery. Through engaging, teaching, and coaching others in thinking from the Three Laws, performance will expand while you discover new and creative applications of the Three Laws. When you take this step, elevating performance has moved from being your personal interest to being the group's interest. At this point, you are onto the opportunity to rewrite the future of an organization—perhaps even to discover an organization's Self and make that the driver of a new era in your company.

We now turn to a set of questions that will guide you on the road to mastering the Three Laws of Performance.

Materials for the Pathway to Mastery

Now that you have a sense of what the pathway to mastery looks like, here are some tools and materials to accelerate your movement—sets of questions to ask and activities to practice.

It's helpful, in this section, if you pick a new performance challenge. The more intractable, long-lasting, and seemingly impossible, the better. Go for something that on the "big deal scale" would be a nine or ten—something that, if resolved, would make a real impact.

First Law Practice: Exploring How the Situation Occurs to You and Others

Look at every facet of the performance challenge you and others face, including actions people have taken or not taken. See the issue in all of its facets. Recall the frustrations, the hopes, the progress you made and didn't make. Recall what people said about the situation, publicly and privately. What explanations and justifications did people use to deal with what didn't work? Feel the stress of the situation, including expectations of other people. Experience the default future that exists for the people involved and how it is influencing the present.

You want to see the various ways in which the present problematic situation is filled up, cluttered, limited in its apparent pathways. We've already talked about how the default future limits and constrains what is experienced as possible in the present. Now let's inquire into how solutions to past problems get placed in the default future.

We call this phenomenon *the problem-solution mass*. The mass develops when the solution to our problem becomes our next problem, which is basically how life goes. For example: You feel lonely. That's a problem. So you fix the problem by getting married. Once the thrill is gone, you realize you have a new problem: it's called "being married." Perhaps the solution is "have a child." Now you have diaper problems, time management problems, and financial problems. You fix that problem by getting a new job, or working hard to get promoted. The problem now is that the job consumes your life, with little time left for the family. At this stage, 50 percent of us give in and solve the problem by getting a divorce. Now there's the return of loneliness, and you have less money. And so it goes: the more we solve our problems, the more problems we have. The French have a saying that captures this paradox: *the more things change, the more they stay the same.*

We are not suggesting that you roll over and not deal with problems. It's just that the fix usually doesn't deal with the underlying issues that need to be handled. Resolving problems means transforming how your situations occur to you and others.

In reflecting on a situation that occurs as needing a performance boost, you might begin by asking (yourself and others), "What is working and what is not working in this situation?" Then, "Is there something that was done in the past to fix a problem that is now here as part of what's not working?" Make a list of all the "business as usual" solutions that people in your industry would use. Or, if the issue is personal, what are the usual actions people take to try to resolve problems like the one you have?

Think of technology, training, appraisals, incentives, decision rights, delegation. Add the management fads. And more staff. More money. What about motivational techniques? Try aphorisms, slogans, posters on the wall highlighting teamwork or courage.

Would any of those *permanently* alter how the issue, and the related situations, occur to you and others?

What if a permanent alteration in this occurring were possible? What could this shift do for performance?

As a side note, notice that this list of "business as usual" solutions is probably what your competitors are doing. If so, doing them moves you to the center of the pack, not to a position of leadership. The essence of competitive advantage is doing different things and doing things differently. At the time of this writing, implementing applications developed from the Three Laws of Performance is so rare that it gives early adopters an edge.

The point to draw from this thought is that the solution to a problem is part of how the situation occurs. Most people are caught in the trap of acting on the solution, which creates the next problem—a cycle they never break. Further, the "business as usual" solutions don't impact how the situation occurs.

Experiencing Correlation: The Hand Dance

In Chapter One, we introduced the notion of correlation but didn't spend much time on it. In fact, this idea is critical to the process of mastering the Three Laws.

The First Law proposes that how a situation occurs to a person doesn't *cause* that person's performance. Nor does the opposite hold true. A person's performance doesn't cause how a situation occurs. Rather, the two correlate. It's like two people dancing. The dance arises in the wholeness of their actions taken together. One dancer doesn't cause the other to move, or else it wouldn't be a dance.

Causation requires a time gap between two actions. Put a drop of acid on a one-celled organism, and milliseconds later, it moves away—irritation causes movement. On the other hand, the latest research from brain science tells us that we (humans, not one-celled organisms) perceive things and act on them *at exactly the same time.* Action happens in our bodies at the same instant that *what is happening?* forms as a pattern in our brain. The two happen simultaneously; therefore, we can't say that one causes the other. They are correlated.

Put your performance challenge on the shelf for a moment. This next exercise, designed to create the experience of correlation, requires a partner. So you will have to involve another person in your reading this book. This is part of the practice of the next chapter, so you are getting a head start here.

Hold your hands up in front of you, palms facing forward, your fingers straight and spread apart. Sit close to your partner, who holds his hands the same way, almost—but not quite—touching your hands.

Designate an "A" and a "B." If a third person is available, she will call out who is to "lead," alternating between A and B: "A," "B," "A," "B," and so on. Otherwise, one of you can act as the caller.

To start the activity, the caller says, "A." That person moves his hands as if across a plane of glass. Up, down, sideways, in circles. The other person follows as best he or she can.

After perhaps ten seconds, the caller says, "B." Now the two of you reverse roles—so that the one who was leading is now following. After ten seconds, reverse roles again when the caller says, "A."

Keep going back and forth, with the caller shortening the time for each round. Eight seconds, then six, then four. Then two, then one.

Then the caller goes back and forth as fast as she can: "ABABABAB." You'll both see that leading and following morph into something that is both and neither. It is a dance, in the true sense.

Once you're done, here are the questions to ask:

- How did you know what the other person was doing, so that you could keep your fingers close but not touching?
- At the beginning, was there a lag time between leading and following? Did this time shrink as the rounds progressed?
- When you hit your stride, together, how long was the lag between leading and following? Most people say there was no lag time at all. If you hit this point, how is it possible for leading and following to happen *at the same time*?
- Was there a point when leading and following became one and the same? If this happened, were you thinking about making it happen or did it just happen?

Here are two explanations. Which one captures the experience of the hand dance?

1. Cause and effect became faster and faster, but even at its full velocity, one of us was causing the other's actions.
2. Cause and effect fell away at some point. A's actions weren't causing B's, nor were B's causing A's. It felt like they were happening at the same time.

Most people say the second explanation captures the experience. That's why this exercise is called the "hand dance"—dancing doesn't occur when you are thinking about where to move your feet (or in this case, hands).

Notice that you have just glimpsed correlation. The movements of one correlated with the movements of the other. There was no cause and effect, no lag time. Your actions, and those of your partner, arose together.

The correlation between you and another person shows what is happening in the movement of life between people. Imagine what lack of grace—what poor performance—would result from someone dancing "by the numbers," or dancing as though his actions caused the actions of his partner. This analogy is worth thinking about. The more you approach a situation using the correlation aspect of the First Law, the greater your access to elevating performance. If you see the correlation between action and the occurring, you'll be able to dance with events as they happen, altering how situations occur to you and others on the fly. People's actions will immediately and naturally "dance" with the new occurring. Performance becomes elegant and graceful.

When you see the powerful connection between performance and how a situation occurs, and you can grok correlation, you are inside the First Law.

Second Law Practice: Exploring How Language Shapes How Things Occur to You

Let's create two categories for any of the phenomena we deal with in work and in life outside of work. One category we call *reality that arises in language* and the other *reality that is independent of language*.

An example of reality that arises in language is marriage. Two people are literally married when a properly designated official pronounces them married. Until that moment they are single individuals; after that moment they are married. A new future is created to live into: being married. All of life changes as a result of altering the occurring between two people.

Another example of something that exists only by virtue of language is *money*. A hundred-dollar bill is the same as a five-dollar bill to your cat—but not to you. The "money" of the bill is in the symbols on the bill, not the paper itself.

Consider the following question: is there anything that occurs to you as totally independent of language? Most people would say "the wall" or "the table." They'll add: "These objects exist whether we have words to describe them or not!"

Maybe not. Consider the table.

There is clearly something there. But labeling and calling the "something there" a *table* carries enormous implications for action. As you label a situation or object, so you behave toward it. With the table, perhaps you dine on it. Perhaps write on its surface. Or create a flower display using its height. Perhaps store books. But you do not place a refrigerator on it.

As human beings, our relationship to the object is inseparable from the language of our terministic screen.

And how do you know it is a table? Because surrounding the table is everything that is *not* the table. But everything that is not the table doesn't exist in reality—negatives are a function of language, not a reflection of reality. We don't know how the table occurs to a dog, but one thing is certain: the dog doesn't refer to it as a table. Perhaps the dog thinks of the table as something to walk around to get to the door, or a place from which the smell of food comes. For us, it's a table. Once we learn language, we can never again see the world without its influence.

To make the point another way: most cultures have a word for dog, and there is something there taking up that physical space (and eating physical food). But in some cultures, people associate *dog* with *friend*. Other cultures associate *dog* with *lunch*. Our experience of the dog, and certainly the dog's experience of us, will be different depending on the language in use.

Going even deeper, physics tells us that solid objects aren't solid at all. They are collections of particles, atoms, separated by vast amounts of empty space. Most of what is out there is literally nothing. "Something is solid" really means for us that we can't go through it and stay intact. But to be able to experience *solid*, we need a word to name it. The name *solid* is not itself solid but allows for solid.

We are not saying that there is nothing "out there" beyond our language. But whatever is beyond our language is not accessible to us. We look at what is out there through our screen of terms—a full set of vocabulary, in which words link to other words—so that *table* and *dog* occur as they do. It's our terministic screen that counts. Once we learn the words for *table* and *wall*, we can't *not* see tables and walls. And as time goes on, other terms get associated with tables and dogs based on experience.

To see the inescapability of the Second Law, take a moment and look around at the physical objects around you. What do they mean to you? Your coffee mug may have a sentimental connection—maybe someone gave it to you—so it occurs as warm and cherished. If you're on an airplane, the experience may occur as busy, chaotic. People around you may occur as happy, or tired, or on the run. Notice that everything around you occurs in a certain way, and that you can't shut it off. Notice, too, that in every case it occurs as it does through language.

We can never see our terministic screen, but we can see its effects. Notice again how people and things around you occur to you. What does this tell you about how life occurs to you? If everything occurs as something to do—a pen occurs as needing to be used, a magazine occurs as needing to be read—perhaps all of life occurs to you as needing to be attended to. Again, all of this is a function of language.

If you're in a discussion group about the Three Laws, we suggest you spend time with others getting at the source of the most important object in language: yourself. How you occur to yourself arises in language, just as with anything else. People who reinvent themselves have the ability to transform how they occur to themselves. (For a guide on group discussion questions, we invite you to visit www.threelaws.com.)

Experiencing Language at Work

Refer back to your performance challenge. Notice that the way the situation occurs and the words used to capture how the situation occurs aren't just connected—they are inseparable.

As you look into how the situation occurs to you, notice connections to past incidents that seem similar and related. See that this situation is tied to other situations, and ways of acting and dealing with past situations are imbedded in actions being taken to deal with this current situation.

Consider also the network of conversations that people have that support and maintain performance the way it is. Even if your challenge is personal—such as losing weight or improving your marriage—there is a network of conversations around you that impacts how that situation occurs to you and others.

Notice:

- What people say
- What people don't say but still communicate
- People's posture, gestures, facial expressions, and tone of voice
- What people write—in e-mails, sticky notes, letters, memos, formal reports, and the like

Consider that you are a node in this network of conversations—much like a node in a network of computers. Notice further that much of this conversation was present before you got there.

Ask these questions:

- How does the situation occur to people, such that people are having these conversations?
- Where are the conversations noisy? Where do they pull in opposite directions?
- Which of the conversations are productive? Which are ineffective?
- What is the relationship between your performance issue and this network of conversations?
- What is the default future that people in this network of conversations are living into?

When you see language at work, and that the way that situations occur arises in language, you are inside the Second Law of Performance.

Third Law Practice: Having a Say About How Situations Occur

You may not be able to change the facts of the situation, but you have something to say about the screen of terms with which you see it. To use our analogy in the first section, you can't change what's in front of you, but you can put in a different set of contact lenses. Once you see the situation in a new way, you'll see opportunities you didn't see before. More to the point, they will occur to you in a new way.

With the power of the Third Law, you can alter how a situation occurs to you. The path to mastery lies in moving as much out of the occurring as is movable. If you have a racket involved with the occurring of this situation, it will color how it occurs to you. To the degree that you give up (through generative language) your rackets as soon as you notice them, you'll be on the path to mastery.

Complete any past issues that are part of this situation, including your relationships with other people.

Commit to seeing the situation, as it is, without the problem-solution mass. If there's any bit of *I've tried this . . .* or *This is really hard*, move those judgments out. See the situation without solutions, without any sense that it's a problem.

Mastery means that there's nothing between you and the thing you're dealing with. If you have knowledge, it's above and behind you, shining light on what you're dealing with. If you have beliefs, expectations, hopes, fears about the situation, mastery means putting these on the shelf so you are not looking through them at what is in front of you.

The masters we have looked at in this chapter don't see problems or bring their past baggage with them. Their commitment is to moving forward, to seeing the situation in a way that allows for elevated performance.

Creating a New Future

If you are using paper to take notes, pull out a new sheet of paper. At the very least, mentally jump to a clean sheet. Consider the following question, about your performance challenge: *How might the situation occur to me, such that my performance would be elevated?* Said in another way, *If this situation occurred to me as [blank], I would be acting in new ways.* Now fill in the blank.

Consider the gap between how situations occur to you now and how they *could* occur to you. What aspects of the occurring, if altered, would make the greatest impact in performance? For example, if a situation that currently occurs to you as dangerous and threatening suddenly occurred to you as something to keep an eye on, would that free you up in what you did and can do?

Consider the network of conversations that supports and maintains how situations occur. What new conversations, if started, would permanently alter how situations occur? What conversations, if removed, would impact how situations occur?

Take a hard look at the network of conversations in light of *integrity*. Do people honor their word? Do they do what is expected, even when they haven't explicitly agreed to do so? Do they communicate honestly, not holding back? How could new conversations be started to begin a cascade of integrity throughout the organization?

Most important, what futures are people living into? Are they inspired by those futures, or resigned to them? Does the future fulfill the concerns of all stakeholders? Is anyone listening for a new future of the organization or group? Who should play that role? How can they be inspired to do so?

Listen to others. What are their concerns? Are those concerns being fulfilled by the future that the organization or group is living into?

What is a new future that would have the stickiness to replace the future people are living into? What future would address everyone's concerns?

Seeing a Situation Through All Three Laws

Return to your performance challenge. Recall how it occurred to you prior to reading this book. How does it occur to you now? Can you see the occurring? Can you see language at work, and the network of conversations? Can you see possible new futures, and how future-based, generative language would rewrite the futures people are living into?

There's a moment for many people when it clicks, when they see situations through the lens of all Three Laws at once. When that happens, things never look the same again. You're now thinking from the Three Laws.

If that hasn't happened yet, take another performance challenge through the questions and activities in this chapter. As you work on a "problem," you will move further down the road to mastery.

If it has clicked, you're now thinking from the Three Laws. The challenge now is to share the Three Laws with others, to engage and involve them in insights that make a difference for them.

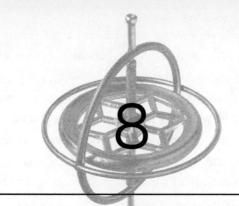

8

Breaking the Performance Barrier

The only thing that matters is performance, and performance comes down to the actions of people. As we've seen in this book, conversations, particularly conversations based in commitment, spark action. In working with thousands of people on implementing the Three Laws, we have identified seven specific commitments that, when made with integrity, reliably break the performance barrier.

Our last piece of advice is this: take on these commitments and let them guide you in the conversations that you have with others.

Commitment 1: Get Out of the Stands

Let's visit a football game in a large stadium. There are people sitting in the stands and people on the field. Everyone is talking, but the conversations in the two locations are very different. In the stands, people are talking *about* the game—judging, evaluating, assessing, making excuses for their team, or saying what their team did right, or rationalizing. There is little at stake, little at risk, and their conversations have virtually no impact on the action of the game.

And then there are the conversations the players are having on the field. These conversations not only affect the game, they *are* the game. Someone may say, "Give me the ball and I'll score!" and the next play is begun. Throughout the game, people are communicating in such a way that the team is focused on winning.

The question is, what type of conversations are you having? On the field, or in the stands?

You leave the stands when you stop assessing and judging and instead put something at risk. Communicate in a way that drives action. Make yourself accountable for winning the game.

Having read this book, you are ready to take to the field. So we ask, are you in the game? If not, what are you waiting for? If you are in the game, how can you get others to join you?

Commitment 2: Create a New Game

Imagine that those areas in which you want to elevate performance are all games. A game starts when some influential person uses future-based language and says that something is more important than something else. The inventor of soccer said that scoring more goals is better than scoring fewer goals. The originator of golf said the opposite—making fewer strokes is better than making more strokes.

You make a new game when you declare that something is important. This is what you're putting at stake, and it is what you're holding yourself accountable to. When others commit to the game with you, they join you on the field.

So use future-based language and declare what's important. Say what's not important. Who said you could do this? You did.

Commitment 3: Make the Obstacles Conditions of the Game

We recently heard a salesperson say, "Clients are slow to make decisions—I could sell more if they were faster." She was making the conditions of the game—selling—an obstacle.

This is as absurd as a team that constantly failed to score saying, "We would have won if the field were only ninety yards long instead of a hundred." Or team members complaining, "We would have won if the players on the other side weren't so strong."

If something occurs to you and others as an obstacle, you'll push back by playing on the obstacle's terms. Instead, make the obstacles conditions of the game.

Like it or not, you are playing on a field that is one hundred yards long, against strong players, with clients slow to make decisions. Given these conditions, what will you do to win?

Commitment 4: Share Your Insights

Breakthrough performance becomes possible when you engage others in the insights from the Three Laws by sharing about them.

Sharing is allowing another to participate in what you're experiencing. Some of us have an aversion to sharing that comes from childhood. This probably began with our mothers telling us to share our candy bar with a friend. Then we noticed that we were left with only half a candy bar—not a good deal. We end up holding on to what is important to us so as to not lose any of it.

That may be what happens in world of candy bars, but it's not what happens with experience and commitment. The more you share your experience, and the more you make your commitments public, the more you get back.

If you share your love for another person, your love isn't lessened, it increases. The same is true with your experience of the Three Laws. The more you share it, the more your experience deepens, your insights take hold, and your capacity to achieve breakthrough results increases. Ideas shared grow and spread.

Further, the more you share, the more the environment around you is shaped by the Three Laws, and elevated performance takes hold.

So who do you share with? The people who matter to you and who you need to win the performance game.

It's really simple, but not necessarily easy. All there is to do is to share your experience. What impact is this book making on you? What do you see that you didn't see before?

When you share, other people take on performance challenges with you and form a network. In this community, everyone is learning and working together to achieve what once looked impossible.

Commitment 5: Find the Right Coaching

On the field, there is another role: the coach. The coach isn't in the stands, and he doesn't play the game, either. Still, he risks as much as anyone who takes to the field.

What does the coach do? From the Three Laws, great coaching alters how the situation of the game occurs for the players, especially at the critical moments. The coach will say and do whatever is necessary to win the game. He may motivate or inspire or give information or tell the players exactly what to do. Regardless, every action alters how the game occurs for the players, so that their actions correlate with winning.

As you create a network that takes on breakthrough performance challenges, you will find yourself coaching. So who coaches you? Our advice is to make this book your coach. We promise that if you get stuck, or knocked off your game, somewhere in this book is an insight that will get you back in the game.

If that doesn't work, seek out great coaching by posting your experience in a community of people who, like you, are playing the performance game. You'll find them on www.threelaws.com.

Commitment 6: Start Filing Your Past in Your Past

We need to get the future and the past straightened out, once and for all.

Human beings make a very simple and far-reaching mistake—one that you must not make if you're going to elevate performance. It's really a filing error.

Imagine two filing cabinets, labeled "The Past" and "The Future." From time to time stressful, difficult, or dangerous things happen. When they do, and we survive, we note what worked, taking a photograph of our actions and keeping it on file in case that situation happens again. So you'll have it in the future, you put it in The Future cabinet.

After you've lived through enough of those incidents, the filing cabinet of The Future is full. The irony is that you no longer have a real future. You may find that you're repeating the past, and you are. When something happens, you dip into The Future file and do what your record tells you to do. You do the same things over and over because you've put those files in your future.

So let's get beyond the filing error.

If we emptied everything out from The Future filing cabinet—all the decisions we placed there to deal with what may happen—what would be left in that filing cabinet?

Nothing.

That's the nature of the real future: there's nothing there. What will happen in the real future is uncertain. Tomorrow will become today, but when it does, it will no longer be tomorrow. Tomorrow, as tomorrow, has nothing in it. It's empty, uncertain, unwritten.

As you look into the real future, you see—nothing.

So the bad news is, you're standing in front of nothingness. Certainty is unavailable.

The good news is, you're standing in front of nothingness. You can only create into nothing. A painter can only paint on a blank canvas. You can create a future into nothingness.

As a way of creating this future, speculate about possible futures that are compelling to you, futures that inspire you. The future to be invented, not figured out. It's not a future designed to fix or solve your current problems. It's a future designed to make a difference for you and others.

You have to look into nothingness and declare what can be and what you actually commit to. If you stay in this conversation, you'll never confuse the future and the past again.

Commitment 7: Play the Game as If Your Life Depended on It

Begin the coaching by starting with yourself. Overturn your life sentence. Create a powerful future to live into. Don't fall into the reality illusion. See occurring as what it is.

Experiment with altering the network of conversations that is your company.

You can't mess this up. You're just having a conversation. In basketball, when the ball goes through the hoop, notice what works. When you feel somewhat conversant, look for people who would be willing to create a network of conversations for performance. Ask them if they'd be interested in building a discussion group for new ideas to resolve difficult issues. With the ones who are interested in playing, create a common future together, one that compels and inspires everyone.

People will resist you, because people resist new ideas all the time. Remember, it was the same for Galileo. Don't take it personally. Resistance is like a thunderstorm: when it rains on you, you get wet—but it isn't personal.

You may find yourself resisting your own commitments, making others wrong, and not creating what you know can be. Remember that you can give up anything that doesn't serve you.

When something stops you, ask whether what is happening is "wrong" or "bad." If that is how it is occurring for you, alter the question from "What is wrong?" to "What is missing?" Treat it as a part of the field on which you're playing. Your job is to win in those conditions. There are no obstacles; there are merely conditions of the game.

Now you are back in the game.

Here is our last word. There are no circumstances in business or in life that you can't handle from the Three Laws. No matter what hurdles you have to jump, challenges you have to face, unfamiliar territory you have to cross, you're ready for it.

Play the game passionately, intensely, and fearlessly. But don't make it significant. It's just a game.

Appendix

The Three Laws of Performance and the Leadership Corollaries

First Law of Performance
How people perform correlates to how situations occur to them

Leadership Corollary 1
Leaders have a say, and give others a say, in how situations occur

Second Law of Performance
How a situation occurs arises in language

Leadership Corollary 2
Leaders master the conversational environment

Third Law of Performance
Future-based language transforms how situations occur to people

Leadership Corollary 3
Leaders listen for the future of their organization

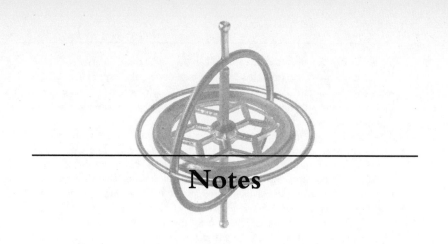

Notes

1. Martin Corboy and Diarmuid O'Corrbui, "The Seven Deadly Sins of Strategy," *Management Accounting* 77, no. 10 (1999): 29–33.
2. Vincent Pellettiere, "Organization Self-Assessment to Determine the Readiness and Risk for a Planned Change," *Organization Development Journal* 24, no. 4 (Winter 2006): 38–44.
3. Helen Keller, *My Religion* (New York: Doubleday, 1928), 20–21. Helen Keller quotation from *My Religion*, courtesy of the American Foundation for the Blind, Helen Keller Archives. Used with permission.
4. Helen Keller quoted in D. B. Updike, *Optimism* (Boston: Merrymount Press), 13.
5. This section draws on work from John R. Searle and John L. Austin, in *Speech Acts* (Cambridge, UK: Cambridge University Press, 1969) and *How to Do Things with Words* (Cambridge, MA: Cambridge University Press, 1969), respectively.
6. This section draws on work from Werner Erhard, Michael C. Jensen, and Steve Zaffron, "Integrity: A Positive Model That Incorporates the Normative Phenomena of Morality, Ethics and Legality,", Harvard Business School NOM Working Paper no. 06–11 (April 25, 2008). Available at http://ssrn.com/abstract = 920625.
7. This section draws on material from "The World Is Your Stage: The Workshop Where Being Meets Acting," a course developed by Werner Erhard and Sanford Robbins.
8. Charles M. Schwab, *Succeeding with What You Have* (Century, 1917; repr., New York: Cosimo Classics, 2005), 39–41.
9. The focus of this chapter is organizations, which can be either for-profit or non-profit. They include institutions, governments, and NGOs, as well as conglomerates, multinationals, even start-up ventures. Corporations are easy to discuss in their legal structure, but the issues they face are faced by organizations of all kinds and sizes. The discussion is just as relevant to newer forms of organization, such as limited liability companies and partnerships.
10. The question of whether animals experience these aspirations often comes up at this point. In this discussion, it's enough to say that even if they experience

love, they can't express it as we can, nor can they label their experience "love." Without the word intermingled into the experience, the experience itself is not the same as ours. It is thus safe to say that our experience of love—and by extension, family, relationships, community, and joy—is uniquely human, and exists by virtue of our language-using nature.

11. The idea of a self-led organization draws its influence, in part, from Warren G. Bennis, "Toward a 'Truly' Scientific Management: The Concept of Organizational Health," *General Systems Yearbook* 7 (1962): 269–82; from the workplace democratization movement, especially Stanley Deetz's *Democracy in an Age of Corporate Colonization: Development in Communication and Politics of Everyday Life* (Albany: State University of New York Press, 1992); and from the self-design literature within organizational development, especially Mohrman and Cummings' *Self Designing Organizations: Learning How to Create High Performance* (Reading, MA: Addison-Wesley, 1990).

12. Cox, La Caze, and Levine, *Stanford Encyclopedia of Philosophy* (originally published April 2001, revised August 2008), http://plato.stanford.edu/entries/integrity/.

13. Erhard, Jensen, and Zaffron, "Integrity" (2008) (see n. 6).

14. This is not a new idea. Similar threads run through the works of major philosophers and psychologists, especially in the twentieth century. Of these, Carl Jung spoke most clearly on the subject; Jung described "coming to selfhood" or "self-realization" as the final step in one's development. According to Jolan Jacobi, in *Psychology of C. G. Jung* (London: Routledge & Kegan Paul, 1942), 127, this process results in "an entirely different attitude toward, and view of, life—in other words a 'transformation' in the fullest sense of the word."

15. This idea draws part of its inspiration from "Stage Five" cultures. See Logan, King, and Fischer-Wright's *Tribal Leadership: Leveraging Natural Groups to Build a Thriving Organization* (New York: HarperCollins, 2008).

16. Some of the information in this section is adapted from "The Ontological Foundations of Leadership and Performance," a course at the Simon School of Business at the University of Rochester, offered in 2006, 2007, and 2008.

17. Douglas Niles and Michael Dobson, *Fox on the Rhine* (New York: Macmillan, 2002), 312.

18. Wilbur Smith, *River God: A Novel of Ancient Egypt* (New York: Macmillan, 1995), 379.

19. Kenneth Burke, *Language as Symbolic Action: Essays on Life, Literature, and Method* (Berkeley: University of California Press, 1968), 114–125. Note: we are taking some liberties with Burke's idea, combining it with aspects of brain science—especially Jeff Hawkins and Sandra Blakeslee, *On Intelligence* (New York: Macmillan, 2005)—and cognitive psychology. Some of what we write was drawn from Appendix B in Logan, King, and Fischer-Wright, *Tribal Leadership*, and three working papers on SSRN by Dave Logan and Halee Fischer-Wright mentioned in that source.

20. Hawkins and Blakeslee, *On Intelligence*, 49.

Acknowledgments

This book wouldn't have been possible without the contribution of many individuals, groups, and organizations.

We acknowledge Landmark Education for making its methodology and body of knowledge available to us. We particularly thank its staff, program leaders, and over one million graduates for their inspiring work.

We thank the editor of this series, Warren Bennis, whose passion for the art and science of leadership has motivated us for years. Warren became a champion of this project almost ten years ago and has guided us throughout the entire process from idea to finished manuscript. We will always be grateful to Warren for his advice, editorial direction, commitment to this project, and vision for what it could become.

We appreciate the support from the faculty and staff of the University of Southern California and the Marshall School of Business. Special thanks go to Tom Cummings, Rich Callahan, Tim Campbell, Jim Ellis, and Steve Sample.

We are thankful to John King, through whom we originally met. As one of Dave's partners in CultureSync, John took on extra work to support this project. Likewise, Jack Bennett took on extra responsibilities to allow for the writing of this book.

In a similar vein, we also acknowledge Fred McWilliams and Jim Kidder, who expanded their daily roles to support Steve.

We appreciate the many experts who gave us their time in interviews, including Chris Ahrends, Ray Anderson, Chris Argyris, Joel Bakan, Geoffrey Bellman, Peter Block, Ray Fowler, Kevin Kelly, Rakesh Khurana, Barney Pell, Lewis Pinault, Bob Rosen, Peter Senge, Monica Sharma, Eraldo Tinoco, Margaret Wheatley, and Dan Yankelovich.

We are indebted to many people who invited us into their companies and, in many cases, told us stories that were very personal. The list includes Lee Browne, Malcolm Burns, Paul Fireman, Antoinette Grib, John Hetrick, Isamu Homma, Michael Jensen, Selinah Makgale, Jorge Mattos, Brad Mills, Akio Nakauchi, Keitaro Nakauchi, Seiko Nakauchi, Arunaraje Patil, Larry Pearson, Laolang Phiri, Mal Salter, Ian Sampson, Don Shelton, Burgess Winter, and Doug Young.

We appreciate our Japanese guides and translators, Yumi Fukushima and Atsuko Ueda, and, for her expert translation of materials, Risako Suzuki Robbins. We also thank Takatoshi Ueno for supporting us in our interviews in Japan.

In South Africa, we acknowledge Mari-Louise Schoeman for arranging and coordinating our interviews at Lonmin.

We recognize the efforts of many people who helped turn rough drafts into this finished book. The list includes Richard Brest, Allan Cohen, Rosalie Dillan, Miriam Diesendruck, Joe DiMaggio, Kirsten Fraunces, Virginia Ginsburg, Michael Jensen, Gretchen Knudsen, Mick Leavitt, Olga Loffredi, Harte Logan, Bob Mueller, Maira Navarro, Ann Overton, Brian Regnier, Robert Richman, Sanford Robbins, Rik Super, Diana Toomey-Wilson, and Aaron Zaffron. We also thank Landmark Education's Research, Development, and Design Team for its input.

We acknowledge the contributions of JMW Consulting and especially Jerry Straus. We also acknowledge the contributions of the Insigniam Performance partners: Michael Waldman, Shideh Bina, and Nathan Rosenberg. We also recognize and appreciate a number of other highly effective management consulting firms with whom we have collaborated and whose work has supported the writing of this book.

Some of the material on leadership in this book was developed in what has become a yearly event for the faculty and students of the Simon School of Business at the University of Rochester. We appreciate the positive response and dialogue during class discussions. We especially thank Dean Mark Zupan for his support and advice.

In turning ideas into a final product, we are grateful to our agent, Bob Mecoy, and our executive editor, Susan Williams. We also thank the team at Jossey-Bass, including Rob Brandt, Kristi Hein, Mark Karmendy, Carolyn Carlstroem, and Amy Packard.

For their support of the book, we acknowledge Eileen LaCario, Jennifer Greer, and Linda Graveline.

We appreciate the hundreds of hours contributed by individual members of the Barbados Group, whose names are mentioned in the Authors' Note.

We also thank the staff and consultants of Vanto Group, who demonstrate amazing commitment to their clients, some of which is captured in this book.

For her tireless support, we especially thank Halee Fischer-Wright, who took time away from her medical practice and consulting engagements to manage our collaboration and key aspects of this book. We appreciate her taking all of that on and keeping us focused.

Last, we acknowledge Werner Erhard, the developer of the original ideas on which much of this material is based. We appreciate his commitment, intellectual effort, and support in key aspects of this book.

To the extent that we got it right, we thank all of these individuals. To the extent that we missed the mark, we ask the indulgence of you, the reader.

The Authors

Steve Zaffron is the CEO of Vanto Group, a San Francisco-based consulting firm specializing in designing and implementing large-scale initiatives that elevate organizational performance. Vanto Group has consulted more than three hundred organizations in twenty countries, including Apple, GlaxoSmithKline, Johnson & Johnson, Heinz Northern Europe, Reebok, Northrop Grumman, BHP-Billiton, Petrobras, Telemar Brazil, and Polus Group Japan. A highly experienced international consultant, he has worked with top executives and has led programs for over a hundred thousand people worldwide. Steve has spoken as an expert in organizational transformation at the Harvard Business School, the Simon School of Business at the University of Rochester, and the Marshall School of Business at the University of Southern California.

He is also a senior executive and board member with Landmark Education, where he spearheaded the design of The Landmark Forum, a program which has been attended by more than a million people.

Steve holds a master's degree from the University of Chicago and graduated magna cum laude from Cornell University.

He loves skiing and jogging, has a passion for the martial arts, and plays classical music on the clarinet and jazz on the saxophone. He and his wife live in Miami, Florida. His adult son lives in Los Angeles.

He can be reached at szaffron@threelaws.com.

Dave Logan is on the faculty at the Marshall School of Business at the University of Southern California, where he teaches Management & Organization in the MBA program. From 2001 to 2004 he served as associate dean of executive education. During that time he started dozens of educational programs in companies in aerospace, commercial real estate, financial services, and health care.

Dave is also cofounder and senior partner of CultureSync, a management consulting firm specializing in cultural change and strategy, whose clients include Intel, American Express, Charles Schwab, Prudential, and Health Net, as well as governments and major non-profits throughout the world.

Dave has written three books, including the acclaimed *Tribal Leadership* (2008, with coauthors John King and Halee Fischer-Wright), and his work has been published in many academic and professional journals. He has been interviewed on most major networks, including CNN, Fox, and NBC.

Dave has a Ph.D. in organizational communication from the Annenberg School at USC. He enjoys rock climbing and distance running and is an avid tennis player. He lives in Los Angeles with his wife, Harte, and their daughter.

He can be reached at dlogan@threelaws.com.

Index